The Hunt for Willie Boy

The

INDIAN-HATING AND POPULAR CULTURE

Hunt

for

Willie

Boy

BY

JAMES A. SANDOS

AND

LARRY E. BURGESS

University of Oklahoma Press : Norman and London

For Adrian Fisher,
whose unexpected death prevented
his seeing in print
the Chemehuevi version of the story
that he helped to bring forward.

Published with the assistance of the National Endowment for the Humanities, a federal agency which supports the study of such fields as history, philosophy, literature, and language.

Library of Congress Cataloging-in-Publication Data

Sandos, James A.
    The hunt for Willie Boy : Indian-hating and popular culture / by
James A. Sandos and Larry E. Burgess.
       p.   cm.
    Includes bibliographic references (p.   ) and index.
    ISBN 0-8061-2598-5 (alk. paper)
    1. Willie Boy, 1880 or 81–1909. 2. Paiute Indians—Biography.
3. Chemehuevi Indians—History. 4. Indians of North America—
Public opinion. 5. Public opinion—United States. I. Burgess,
Larry E., 1945– . II. Title.
E99.P2W527 1994
973'.04974—dc20   93-11952
                                                CIP

Text design by Cathy Carney Imboden.

The paper in this book meets the guidelines for permanence and durability of the Committee on Production Guidelines for Book Longevity of the Council on Library Resources, Inc. ∞

1 2 3 4 5 6 7 8 9 10

This reappraisal is not meant to make white Americans "look bad." The intention is, on the contrary, simply to make it clear that in western American history, heroism and villainy, virtue and vice, nobility and shoddiness appear in roughly the same proportions as they appear in any other subject of human history (and with the same relativity of definition and judgment). This is only disillusioning to those who have come to depend on illusions.

—Patricia Nelson Limerick,
"What on Earth Is the New
Western History?"

Getting the facts straight is only the first step in any reconstruction of the past, but it is a necessary step and by no means an easy one. . . . I do not doubt that fiction of the highest quality and history of the highest quality can be written by the same person, but I question whether both can be incorporated into the same book.

—Don. E. Fehrenbacher,
commenting on Gore Vidal's
*Lincoln, American
Historical Review*

Contents

List of Illustrations ix

Preface xi

Acknowledgments xv

1. Introduction: Crises and Approach 3

2. The White Man's Willie Boy in the Press 18

3. The White Man's Willie Boy in Non?-Fiction 36

4. The White Man's Willie Boy in Hollywood 54

5. A Different White Man's Willie Boy 72

6. Trying to Enter a Numinous Land 87

7. A Simple Story Retold 112

8. How Willie Boy Recovered His Song 114

9. Conclusion 128

Appendix. Willie Boy: Published Accounts 136

Notes 145

Bibliography 162

Index 171

Illustrations

FIGURES

1. Willie Boy wanted poster, 1909   26

2. Posseman during Willie Boy manhunt
   wearing handcuffs on hip, 1909   28

3. Message allegedly written by
   Carlota/Isoleta Mike during flight   40

4. The monument to law enforcement at the
   Willie Boy suicide site   51

5. Photograph of Willie Boy in county jail
   suit, ca. 1906   67

6. Photograph of Willie Boy in Banning
   before incident, 1909   104

7. Photograph of Wovoka, source of the
   1890 Ghost Dance revival   105

8. Photograph of Ruby Mountain ambush
   site from Willie Boy's view   124

9. Photograph of food tins found at Willie
   Boy ambush site, ca. 1958   125

MAP

1. Locator map of communities in the story,
   with inset of Banning and environs   2

Preface

On November 15, 1991, a drizzling, gray day, we drove the two hundred miles from southern California out to the river. We arrived midmorning at the library of the Colorado River Indian Tribes (CRIT) Reservation in Parker, Arizona. Four tribes share the space—Mojave, Chemehuevi, Navajo, and Hopi. We were there to meet with some of the Chemehuevi tribal elders, who had the library's small meeting room to themselves. We were there to review the draft of this book with them, to insure that we had presented their words accurately.

We knew four of the people fairly well. Adrian Fisher, former head of the Tribal Council and early member of the U.S. Army's Special Forces, moving deliberately with his cane, chatted with Mary Lou Brown as he slipped into a plastic chair next to her. Mary Lou was clearly the oldest in the group. Next to her was another woman whom we had not met before. Next to her sat Patrick Lyttle, looking up as though he were listening to all and none of the conversations around him. He had recently been sick and may have been in some pain.

Alberta Van Fleet talked animatedly with a man sitting next to her who was unknown to us. At the edge of the group, pouring coffee, stood a young woman whom Adrian introduced to us as a niece. Since she worked in the library, she went off to attend to other patrons when she finished preparing the drinks.

We had sent copies of our writings to each of the four in advance and, after several minutes of conversation, asked if anyone had anything to add or change. Adrian's manuscript was out of order so we repaginated it. Mary Lou said that she did not think she was yet eighty-two. We replied that that was the age she had given us, to which she answered that we may not have heard it right but at least we had listened. One by one, each of them who had talked to us on earlier visits spoke around the table. No comment was addressed to the content of our writing but only to the story itself or to its consequences.

At one point Adrian asked, "What happens now?" We said that if they agreed, we would seek an academic publisher for our manuscript. "How long will that take?" We allowed that we did not know and, given the subsequent history of the manuscript, it was good that we did not suggest a publication date. Alberta said she just wanted something for her grandson to read in school that showed another version of Willie Boy.

Mary Lou's voice, high but firm, announced to the table, "Wolf and Coyote went out one day to find something really good to eat . . . ," and with that she began to tell an ancient Chemehuevi legend. Telling the story is important for the Chemehuevi, as it is for most Indian peoples; impatient non-Indians want the plot summary. So here it is. The father of Wolf and Coyote, Gato, promised both sons that one day they would have a place in the Rainbow. After she continued the tale for a while, she paused. "Oh, I can't say that next part," Mary Lou giggled. "Its too dirty." We claimed to have said or heard or told some pretty dirty things and said that we would not be offended. In fact, we said, we were quite curious. "No, I can't tell you that. But I'll tell you something else." She continued. Coyote killed Wolf in jealousy and buried Wolf's body. When he was asked by Gato where his brother was, Coyote lied and claimed he did not know. When Coyote went back to look at the body it was gone, even the blood. When he looked up, Coyote saw the Rainbow and recognized Wolf in the red color of his blood. Yet Gato did not forget his promise, and now, when you look at the Rainbow, you can see Coyote; he is at the bottom, the white mist you almost miss. "We have to go now," Mary Lou said abruptly. "We have been sitting so long that our butts have all gotten wrinkled and if we don't stand up our butts will sag. That's what happens from too much sitting."

As we rose and moved away from the table Adrian said to Patrick, "You know, I've heard that story many times but I don't remember hearing this version of it." "Me neither," replied Patrick.

As we left the library we stopped to speak to Adrian's niece. We thought she should invite Mary Lou back to tape record the story and to include the dirty part that Mary Lou would not tell us but might tell a Chemehuevi audience. The young woman looked us over carefully. "Mary Lou told you an old story, huh?"

Outside in our car, opposite the library parking strip, we pulled behind Adrian's vehicle, waiting to follow him to the restaurant where we were taking the elders to lunch. As we talked about the meeting, we gradually realized that we had just participated in a ceremony.

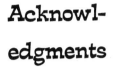

Acknowledgments

Curiously enough, this project had its origins in a rejection, and it encountered others on its way to eventual completion. We had responded to a call from the National Endowment for the Humanities to promote humanities public programming through a joint venture involving a public and university library centered on a theme distinctive to the community in which the libraries were located. After attending an NEH sponsored workshop on how to write the proposal, at the agency's urging, we submitted a program that included, in part, a reading of Harry Lawton's *Willie Boy: A Desert Manhunt*, followed by the screening of the film made from it, *Tell Them Willie Boy Is Here*. NEH staff members, with whom we had consulted at each step in proposal development, professed genuine enthusiasm for the project. Yet it was rejected by NEH expert panels not once, but twice.

In the process of working on the proposal we became impressed with Lawton's novel and its potential relationship to historical inquiry. Hence the NEH rejections, instead of discouraging us, impelled us to probe the incident more deeply and to focus on a historical investigation of the episode. Thus our first intellectual acknowledgment is to Harry Lawton and his gripping novel.

Frederick Hoxie, director of the D'Arcy McNickle Center for the Study of the American Indian at the Newberry Library, gave us our first public forum for presenting some of our historical inquiry at the 1989 annual meeting of the American Society for Ethnohistory held in Chicago. His comments encouraged us to continue. The following year Donald Grinde (Yamasee), then Rupert N. Costo Chair in Native American Studies at the University of California at Riverside, encouraged us to report on our fieldwork among the Chemehuevi at the California Indian Conference that he hosted in 1990. From an academic perspective, Fred and Don helped to get our project launched.

At one point we thought what we had was an article and submitted a manuscript to the *Journal of American History*. Its editor, David Thelen, proved a model of graciousness in declining the paper; we realized that it needed to be expanded into a short book. In the review process, one of the readers, Richard Drinnon, asked to be identified to us. That introduction began a correspondence that has been of inestimable value to our work. Richard's tough-minded criticisms and probing questions sent us back to the books and further into the field than we had ventured thus far. There was irony in our interaction, for we had both been influenced by his *Facing West* as we grappled with the power of Indian-hating in shaping popular culture. The Chemehuevi elders who helped us in California and Arizona, whose words we present in the book, we acknowledge in the order in which we met them: Joe Benitez, former Tribal Chairman at Cabazon Indian Reservation in Indio, California; Adrian Fisher, former head of the Tribal Council at the Colorado River Indian Tribes Reservation at Parker, Arizona; Alberta Van Fleet; Mary Lou Brown; and Patrick Lytle. Without their cooperation the book would not exist.

In 1935, journalist Willard S. Wood offered the first map of the Willie Boy manhunt. Although it was an approximation of the route whites thought Willie Boy had taken, other journalists have presented it with slight variations in successive tellings (appendix entries 2, 4, 11, and 24). Continuing that practice by including Willie Boy's route on our own map would only perpetuate the problems we seek to correct. Thus we offer only a cultural relief rather than another white-imposed projection of Willie Boy's track.

The assistance provided by the Archives at the A. K. Smiley Public Library in Redlands and by the staffs of the George and Verda Armacost Library at the University of Redlands, along with the Special Collections Department of the University of California at Riverside, the Sherman Library at Corona del Mar, the Laguna Niguel branch of the National Archives, and the National Archives in Washington, D.C., deserve recognition. Sandi Ritchie of the Armacost did simply amazing things with interlibrary loan in locating obscure references for us; Janice Jones of the Smiley lent valuable assistance in scheduling.

Scholars who write owe special gratitude to spouses who endure. Tish Sandos and Charlotte Burgess both encouraged and tolerated our trips, our talk, and the time-consuming elements of collaboration. We thank them.

John Drayton made this project a University of Oklahoma Press book; Sarah Nestor shaped the final text. Robert Berkhofer and James Rawls read and commented thoughtfully on a draft, suggesting revisions that have strengthened the work. These four people helped us to complete our obligation to the Chemehuevi Tribal Elders. While we acknowledge and appreciate our debt to others, we alone, together, are responsible for what is contained herein. We will take whatever blame or praise may come.

The
Hunt for
Willie Boy

Locator map of the communities involved in this story, from Los Angeles in the west to Parker, Arizona, in the east. The inset shows Banning and its environs. We have not reproduced Willie Boy's route because other attempts to do so have been nothing more than white projections of where they thought he went. Cartography by Bill Nelson.

1

Introduction:
Crises and
Approach

Historically, this book is a retelling of an episode of local history in California, both trivialized and mythologized in print over eight decades and raised to national significance because Robert Redford starred in a film about it. Our scholarship employs traditional historical methods plus ethnohistory, the combination of anthropology with our discipline, to create a historical ethnography that seeks to explain how the traditional version came into being and has been perpetuated for over eighty years. We have derived inspiration from Roy Harvey Pearce and Richard Drinnon, whose reflections upon what Herman Melville called the metaphysics of Indian-hating have alerted us to the biases against trying to bring previously excluded peoples into the writing of history. We have, ironically, undertaken our task at a time when history in America is undergoing another in a series of identity crises.

As the twentieth century closes, the American historical profession finds itself in a crisis that has plagued it, with varying intensity, for nearly one hundred years. Crisis symptoms, we are told, are to be seen in the proliferation of specialized studies since the 1960s, the emergence and rise of various scholarly themes — women's history, black and ethnic studies, public history, environmental history — to challenge older patterns of historical explanation and to clamor for center stage in telling the nation's past. Stories that have previously been on the periphery of historical study now demand to become the center; the center, as the growing number of ever-more-specialized research indicates, no longer holds.[1]

Concern with symptoms, however, masks the cause of the crisis. Peter Novick, in his book *That Noble Dream,* locates that cause in the collapse of the notion that history was a science, or at least employed a scientific methodology, to seek an ultimate truth. The "objectivity question," as Novick phrases it in his subtitle, has been the central issue in the American historical profession for a century. Advocates of objectivity have claimed that a sharp distinction exists between historical facts and their interpretation by a supposedly disinterested observer; that precise knowledge of the past could be established by employing the methods of science to do empirical research; and that the results of such investigations were true and value free. Critics of objectivity have argued that the distinction between object and observer is artificial and that no absolute truth can be determined. The result of this criticism has been a relativism in which one viewpoint is as good as another. As the relativists have ascended within the profession, we have come to the point of "every group its own historian," in the words of one of Novick's chapter titles.

The crisis has affected nearly every subfield, and 5 American Indian history, to which our research belongs, is no exception. Those who wrote what Robert Berkhofer has called the New Indian History sought to combine anthropological data on Indian cultures with the written documents of history, to write ethnohistory from an Indian perspective. In the elaboration of the subfield, however, cultural pluralism has nearly given way to Indian ethnocentrism.[2]

For ethnohistorian Calvin Martin, the crisis in the subfield over what could be known about the past brought him to a disturbing conclusion: he reluctantly decided that Indians can never be part of history because history is defined by European norms. History is white, linear, and concerned with "anthropological," or Western, ethics and time.

Indians, argues Martin, are "biological" rather than "anthropological" in their worldview. Indians focus on the relationship between humans and their environment in contrast to the anthropological focus upon relations among humans. Thus Indians conceptualize "time" and "history" in such radically different ways as to make null any discussion of Indians within history as it has generally been written. To write a truer story of the Indian past, Martin argues, historians would have to shed their absorption with anthropological time and locate themselves instead within the Indians' biological sense of time. The bridge for doing that, he supposed, would be poetry.[3]

While accepting much of Martin's observations and warnings, we nevertheless disagree with his conclusion. We think that a way to present Indians on their own terms can be realized short of poetry and the author-created object that is the poem. In the particular story that we will present, Indians have told us their version of events explicitly to correct prevailing white views that to them are wrong. In this instance traditional tribal peoples want their story told in the white world; they know it involves telling the story in a white or Western way. Ironically, native people are seeking to be heard in white history at the very moment when that history is plagued by self-doubt over what can possibly be known.

A way out of this dilemma confronts Martin and is described by Novick. To James T. Kloppenberg, Novick has drawn too sharp a distinction between the objectivity issue and relativism; in the process he has lost sight of a different path. Kloppenberg observes that most historians writing since the early twentieth century have been heavily influenced by the thinking of William James and John Dewey. According to Kloppenberg,

> As James understood and Dewey reaffirmed, there is in pragmatic theory a fruitful alternative to relativism. Hypotheses—such as historical interpretations— can be checked against all available evidence and subjected to the most rigorous critical tests the community of historians can devise. If they are verified provi-

sionally, they stand. If they are disproved, new interpretations must be advanced and subjected to similar testing. The process is imperfect but not random; the results always tentative but not worthless.[4]

We propose to employ the "pragmatic hermeneutics" described by Kloppenberg as a vehicle for moving out of the cul-de-sac envisioned by Martin. As America confronts the quincentenary of what Alfred Crosby has called the Columbian exchange, we think it self-evident that Indians must be sensitively included in telling the history of the multicultural world Columbus left in his wake. Many of the New Indian historians have done that and exhorted others to do likewise.[5] That in some instances it has taken five hundred years to include Indians in this story makes their incorporation now all the more imperative.

The story we bring forward has never before been treated by historians. More than eighty years ago, on the deserts of Southern California, a drama unfolded involving conflict among Indians. Given the time and place, an Indian quarrel between Willie Boy and his potential father-in-law ought to have remained private. Yet that conflict led to posse pursuit—aided by Indian trackers—of the young Indian, Willie Boy, for crimes allegedly committed against American law. The white pursuit was heavily influenced by the press, the coincidental visit of an American president, and the journalistic speculation that the Indian fugitive might become a presidential assassin. In the din of white storytelling Willie Boy's voice became lost, his personal version or song ignored as the white account became the public and known version.

After the clamor of the moment had passed, the story of Willie Boy passed into local white lore as an example to teach others about the law and justice of the West. The story was compact. On Sunday evening, September 26, 1909, a Paiute Indian named Willie Boy drank too much stolen whiskey, then stole a rifle and went to the temporary camp of William Mike, a Chemehuevi, located in an orchard on the Gilman Ranch in Banning.

Willie Boy first killed the old man in his sleep and then kidnapped William Mike's fourteen-year-old daughter, Carlota.[6] They were pursued by a posse of white locals aided by Indian trackers from the nearby Morongo Reservation. In the course of the pursuit Willie Boy killed the girl when she slowed his flight, then he took off across the desert. For unknown reasons he later returned to the scene of his crime against her, where he encountered and ambushed another posse at Ruby Mountain. In the course of the skirmish he wounded a white man. As they were taking their wounded comrade to safety, the possemen heard a single shot, from the direction of the supposedly exhausted Willie Boy. A week later, yet another posse found the cause: Willie Boy had committed suicide with his last bullet. Willie Boy's violence exemplified a "return to savagery" of a supposedly assimilated Indian whose rampage was properly dealt with by the forces of law and order.

This story for local whites in Southern California hardly remained local. In 1960 journalist Harry Lawton published his so-called nonfiction novel *Willie Boy: A Desert Manhunt,* devoting its two hundred

8

pages to the saga primarily from the perspective of the posse. For him this was "the last great manhunt in the Western tradition," making it instantly part of the mythic West. The posse then became the agents of "civilization" bringing the evil and unruly savage Indian to justice. To ensure accuracy, he assured his readers, he had done research in Bureau of Indian Affairs records, interviewed possemen and their descendants, checked pertinent court records, and read press accounts of the time. Lawton explained that he "used a reconstructional approach in telling the story of Willie Boy. At the same time I have distorted no hard fact."[7] Later, he elaborated further. "Although it probably makes no real difference to the reader, throughout the book trains run at the right time and the moon is up at the right time. It made a difference to me."[8] Such claims to accuracy increased the credibility of Lawton's version of the tale, making of it a kind of official story.

9

Lawton sold the film rights, and Abraham Lincoln Polonsky made *Tell Them Willie Boy Is Here,* released in 1969, starring Robert Redford, Katherine Ross, and Robert Blake as Willie Boy. Despite major differences between the book and the film, Lawton pronounced himself happy with the final result, remarking that "Polonsky picked up on the hidden refrains throughout the book . . . and, in a sense, it was a way for me to do it again."[9]

Thus in a decade, the Willie Boy tale for local whites in a remote area of Southern California became part of the national myth of the West. Through the vehicle of a "nonfiction novel" told as an "existential Western" and translated onto the screen, the story has entered popular culture as a "cult film," forever associated with Robert Redford.[10] Through national and international distribution, as well as television playtime, the Willie Boy story has reached and continues to reach millions of viewers.

10   What that story tells people is an aspect of the subject we wish to explore because the film is part of the Western genre, with its own dynamic and logic, that contributes to a preservation of the white version of the frontier and perpetuates Indian-hating. In our inquiry we are concerned with recovering a past that reveals the nuances of time, place, and motivation—a past sensitive to cultural differences that novels and films, especially when dealing with Indians, frequently omit. Although *Tell Them Willie Boy Is Here* reverses Lawton's praise of the posse, the film is still another white fable about the Indian, a cautionary story about the "other" designed to show the superiority of the white teller while using the Indian as foil to criticize American society.

A perspective of the Indians involved in this story has not been presented by whites, but the events cannot be adequately interpreted without one. Moreover, recovering an Indian perspective requires a more careful reconstruction of the white record than has previously been presented; it also requires developing an appreciation of the role of Indian spirituality in this story and a willingness to allow a worldview in which alternative explanation is possible.

Our approach has yielded a historical ethnography that helps to explain this story from an Indian as well as a white perspective. It is an attempt to address the concerns about the differences between biological and anthropological time that trouble Calvin Martin. The results of our investigation, which draws upon both Indian and white sources, contradict most alleged facts in the standard story and challenge virtually all of the imputed motivation of the various actors. By our informal count, the Willie Boy story has been told in print thirty-four times from 1926 to 1991 (see Appendix), yet ours is the first study by professional historians. The story that we found is more intricate and its meaning more important than anything yet presented.

The episode's importance largely lies in the insight the history of this story provides into what Herman Melville called the metaphysics of Indian-hating in his 1857 novel *The Confidence Man*. For Melville, the "Indian-hater *par excellence*" was the backwoodsman who combined the negative attitudes toward Indians generally prevailing in the community with "his private passion," an affront real or imagined, to make a vow "the hate of which is a vortex from whose suction scarce the remotest chip of the guilty race may feel reasonably secure." Much of the work of the Indian-hater par excellence was done away from the city or town, in the vast depths of Indian territory, where it was little seen by other whites.

Melville went on to suggest that insights into the Indian-hater par excellence could be derived from studying the "diluted Indian-hater" whose "heart proves not so steely as his brain."[11] Both of these types can be discerned in the history of the Willie Boy

tale. By bringing the Willie Boy episode into historical discourse, we can begin the process of countering
the Indian-hating that the prevailing story perpetuates. The concept of the metaphysics of Indian-hating
raises the disturbing possibility that those who pro-
fess not to hate Indians and even native peoples
themselves can inadvertently be sucked into the vortex.[12]

12

We are aware of the potential biases posed by our
gender, age, sexual preference, and religious background. As will become apparent in reading this
book, we have attempted to correct for these biases.
But there is a subtle legacy of Christianity that we
need to acknowledge at the outset, namely, the de-
spiritualization of the land.

The spread of Christianity across Europe sought
the decline of "paganism," the Christian term used to
describe those who had not heard or accepted its
teachings. Christianity sought the triumph of one God
over many, the substitution of specific worship places—
churches—for sacred sites scattered across the land.
By the fifteenth century, Christianity had largely
banished the spirits of the earth from groves, caves,
rocks, streams, and windy points; Christianity had
despiritualized the natural world.[13] By the time Europeans "found" America, they had been Christianized
for so long that they were unaware of the spiritual land
of the aboriginal, pagan world.

Europeans, completely unfamiliar with Indians,
did not associate the American land with existing
supernatural sites. To Europeans, America was a
place of limitless lands, mineral riches, and potential

converts; America was a terrain without supernatural mystery or sacred sites, a land inhabited by pagans of a different color. To Europeans, those differences in religion and color constituted inferiority, and Europeans largely believed that they had nothing to learn from an inferior people. As Roy Harvey Pearce aptly phrased it, "Indian-hating is thus subsumed under a larger metaphysics, that of Christian, civilized progress."[14] What this means is that to understand an episode in Indian history, especially one involving the close relationship between people and land, the investigator must seek to learn from Indians themselves the meaning of the sacred.

In our presentation, we use as a base the reporting on the case carried in the local press, those newspapers published in Riverside and San Bernardino counties. That material composes most of the second chapter. We have also studied the regional press, those newspapers published in Los Angeles, and some newspapers in the Midwest and East that claimed a large, urban readership. In each case we see that bigotry and racism, along with sensationalism and exaggeration, characterize much, but not all, of the writing. As with any other texts, we have culled only materials that can be corroborated from other sources; discrepancies, inconsistencies, and blatant racism in the coverage is noted.

In chapter 3 we describe how the story of the manhunt developed over the years, showing how the various tellers shaped the tale for their audiences. We discuss Lawton's book at length because, although only eleventh among the thirty-four published versions, it synthesized local lore with regional reporting and has influenced subsequent tellings. We show how the current Willie Boy Days sale and celebration in Landers, California, perpetuates Indian-hating.

In the fourth chapter we examine how the film was made with specific reference to the development of scenes crucial to convey the white man's story. By comparing the evolution of select scenes through three different script versions, with the final shot before camera, we hope to reveal insight into the process by which narrative becomes visual symbol and sometimes stereotype. We devote a separate chapter to this subject because the film version is the most widely known and, like Natalie Zemon Davis in her concern for going beyond the film treatment of Martin Guerre,[15] we hope to demonstrate that a richer story lies beyond the camera's view.

In the fifth chapter we present an alternate white view of Willie Boy based upon our analysis, as historians, of all the available evidence from white sources. To do that, we have had to show explicitly how the frontier myth has subtly shaped the view of events that has prevailed for over eight decades. Our corrective is based upon previously unavailable materials from the records of the Bureau of Indian Affairs, Bureau of the Census, Department of Justice, and Department of War. We scrutinized little-used local records from the coroner's and sheriff's offices as well as the personal collections of Harry Lawton at the University of California at Riverside and of his publisher, Horace Parker, at the Sherman Library in Corona del Mar.

To go beyond even the revised white view, we had to try to enter the land as the Chemehuevis saw it, for they were the Indian group to which Willie Boy principally belonged. We had to inquire into Chemehuevi culture, myth, spiritual thought, and religious revival. In the physical world, to help us understand how Willie Boy survived, we had to learn the significance of the modern Chemehuevi observation: "To the white man, the desert is a wasteland; to us, it is a supermarket."[16] In the Chemehuevi spiritual world, we had to learn the importance of the Ghost Dance for Willie Boy.

We were aided in our inquiry by contact with several Chemehuevis, women and men, who talked to us about their past. Family members from both Willie Boy's clan and the Mike/Boniface clan decided to converse openly with us to bring out their side of the story. During our conversations we discerned both oral history (an account of events seen by an observer) and oral tradition (family lore preserved over a generation or more). Especially by talking to Chemehuevi women, we gained insight into this story that might have otherwise been lost because of a subtle gender bias.

We are aware that the crisis affecting the historical profession has a counterpart in ethnography. David Murray has succinctly recounted that crisis, noting that some way must be found to move beyond the traditional practice of a scholar writing up her or his field notes in such a way that the observer's presence in the writing is erased and the resultant picture of native life is left as disembodied authority. We describe our work in Chemehuevi ethnography in chapter 6 and, following some thoughts of Murray,[17] present our findings as a dialogue between contemporary Chemehuevis and printed ethnographies to develop a historical ethnography pertinent to this incident. In chapter 7 we attempt to tell a version of the story in a Chemehuevi style.

16 In Chemehuevi tradition, as in all cultures, important myths are retold for their value in recalling for tribal members their collective past and for inculcating proper behavior among the young. One such tale is called "How Wildcat Brothers Recovered Their Hunting Song."[18] It suggested the title of chapter 8, "How Willie Boy Recovered His Song," in which we attempt to present the song sung by Willie Boy that has been denied by white storytellers. It is important to know that in Chemehuevi myth a protagonist uses magic, animal friends, and other people to secure a goal. This Chemehuevi practice must be understood lest it be thought that somehow we, and not Willie Boy, are recovering his song.

By acknowledging our potential biases, using varied methodologies, and presenting multiple perspectives, we are attempting a different kind of history. Ours is still in the tradition of "pragmatic hermeneutics," but the role of inference in piecing together the story of native peoples means that the hypotheses we advance will push to expand Western standards of proof. We seek to suggest a way of reconciling anthropological and biological time. To move beyond Indian-hating requires an attempt at recognizing another method of explanation, one in which historical ethnography can be pertinent.

The relevance of this telling of the Willie Boy story from multiple perspectives becomes compelling as Americans face the quincentenary of the beginning of the Columbian voyages. The European-dominated view of the multicultural New World that has arisen since Columbus has ill prepared Americans to confront the issues of cultural diversity that, five centuries later, demand to be addressed. It is in the spirit of trying to understand one another by respecting our cultural differences and acknowledging our shared humanity that we offer our own work here.

17

2

The White Man's Willie Boy in the Press

The contemporary newspaper coverage of the Willie Boy story constitutes the raw data for historical analysis; unfortunately for historians, however, newspapers are problematic sources. While Thomas Holt did the main reporting for the *San Bernardino Sun* and his junior colleague James Guthrie reported as a stringer for the *Los Angeles Herald,* neither received credit for his account. With the exception of the reporting of Randolph Madison, who joined the last posse and so entered the story late, no reporter received a byline for his stories.[1]

Some newspapers relied on the same reporter or copied dispatches in whole cloth. Hence much of what was written was anonymous, embellished by rewrite men in a home office, the printed version reflecting two or more layers of telling. Since the purpose of the stories was to sell papers by generating reader interest, much of the language is exaggerated, and most of it reflects the white racism prevalent at the time. Within the context of Indian-hating, local and regional newspapers reported any sensational story about Indians without regard to its internal logic or plausibility.

What we bring to a reading of the newspapers that others have not is a careful comparative study of the press. We have identified common threads in reporting the story, most of which are factually wrong, and use the accounts as a gauge of accuracy. We use whatever reporting can be confirmed from collateral sources or seems authentic based upon custom or because it is a direct quote from a governmental official who could sue the paper if the report were false. Local papers that we studied that covered the event included: the *Redlands Daily Facts* and the *Redlands Daily Review,* both of which were among the most accurate; although the *Banning Record,* the *San Bernardino Daily Sun,* and the *Riverside Morning Mission* carried more lurid accounts, they nonetheless included important details.

The regional papers in Los Angeles were important as well, and we examined particularly the *Herald,* the *Express,* and the *Daily Times.* Madison worked for the *Record,* but because fire destroyed back copies, a run of that paper for the period has been impossible to find. We have thus used Madison's reports as conveyed in other papers or from the files of the Newspaper Enterprise Association, with which he placed some stories. We have subjected Madison's accounts to the same scrutiny that we used on the others. We have also checked coverage in other newspapers in California, Illinois, Missouri, New York, and Washington.

THE SETTING

Banning and its environs, the starting point of the story, lie in Southern California, approximately eighty-five miles inland from Los Angeles and twenty-three miles west of Palm Springs. Banning, situated in the San Gorgonio Pass, was created by the Southern Pacific Railroad, which used it as a water stop for its trains. Although the railroad ran through Indian land, Southern Pacific claimed its customary right to alternating sections of land along the railbed. The railroad then sold property to a syndicate of Nevada investors that in turn laid out the town site in 1884–85. The syndicate chose the location because it had the best water supply between Yuma, Arizona, and Colton, California.[2]

Indians lived in the area before white settlers arrived, and tension between the two groups followed shortly after contact. When the Malki Reservation, later and more commonly known to whites as Morongo, was established in 1888, several families of settlers were evicted by U.S. Army troops. Among those put off Indian land were the families of Ben de Crevecoeur, distinguished locally as the first white baby born in the pass area, and the Josts. The two families merged after C. F. Jost married the widow Margaret de Crevecoeur two years following the murder of her husband by another settler.[3]

In 1890 a presidential commission headed by Albert K. Smiley, New York philanthropist and reformer of Indian affairs, was given the task of creating the reservation boundaries for Southern California, which have largely persisted until the present. When the commissioners visited Morongo the following year, they found "much trouble." Approximately a hundred Indians were surrounded and in some cases made into enclaves by the three hundred white settlers.

"To state the situation briefly," the commissioners wrote, "we found the Indians the acknowledged holders of lands they did not want or work, and the whites insisted upon rights to lands that are absolutely essential to the Indians, if a [viable] reservation is to be established here."[4] Among those pressing claims against the federal government for unlawful dispossession were the Josts.

Another person causing the Indians difficulty was Lucy Ann Toutain, a widow who had borne eleven children and who lived on ten acres inside the reservation. The commissioners described her as "a woman who has given the Indians and the Indian Agent much trouble" because she had promised verbally to sell the property to the Indians but signed nothing.[5]

"We fear," the commissioners noted, "if the claims of these . . . parties are pressed to a hearing in the various courts, the result will be very disastrous to the Indians as affecting their rights to both water and land."[6] Caution became the watchword, and Indian-white tensions persisted while cases languished in the courts. Smiley sadly concluded, "Race prejudice is too strong in southern California to secure a fair administration of justice."[7]

The Indians at Morongo were caught with land unsuitable for dry farming and little access to water. Twenty years later they were deep in economic and personal depression. Following a lengthy period of neglect by the Bureau of Indian Affairs, "the agency had run down; the liquor evil had become a scourge"; and local whites described the Indians to Indian Commissioner Francis Leupp as "good for nothing."[8]

Leupp knew that the Morongo agency needed help. "After studying my field staff over thoroughly," Leupp "decided that the very man" to do the job "was Miss Clara True. I gave her a man's work," he observed, "and she has done it better than any man who has been in there for thirty years." Leupp described her as a member of his "Amazonian contingent,"[9] capable of coping with any problem. When she arrived at Morongo, however, Clara True looked around and "decided to resign."[10] She reconsidered, however, and stayed, confirming Leupp's faith in her.

Her immediate supervisor described her as "a woman 40 years of age, small in stature but strong and wiry, with an indomitable will and courage, thoroughly able to handle the Indians and all questions arising in connection with her work."[11] She attacked the bootleggers with increasingly greater effect. She opposed alcohol itself, not just its impact upon Indians, and she enlisted the aid of celebrated saloon breaker William E. "Pussyfoot" Johnson to drive alcohol peddlers from the reservation and its environs.[12]

22

The Hunt for Willie Boy

Clara True simultaneously sought to improve Indian agriculture. She had the Indians sink a concrete tunnel into the water-bearing strata from which their small trickle of water emanated, thereby increasing the flow. This tactic increased available irrigation water, permitting land to be reclaimed; the number and size of Indian cultivated fields began to grow within a few months of her appointment.

23

By late 1908 she had so many Indians tending to their own fields that she had created a labor shortage for neighboring white farmers.[13] The local labor shortage opened opportunities for Indians further out on the desert to migrate into Banning for seasonal employment working fruit and harvesting cereals. Thus by late summer 1909 a group of desert Chemehuevi from Twentynine Palms came to Banning seeking work.

THE EVENTS FROM A WHITE PERSPECTIVE
The immediate events began around 9:00 P.M. the night of September 26, 1909, when Willie Boy went to the camp of the man known to whites as Old Mike or Mike Boniface, located among the cottonwood trees adjacent to a creek on the Gilman Ranch in Banning. The man's name actually was William Mike, but the names Mike and Boniface were used interchangeably by whites.[14] The entire Mike/Boniface family, who were Chemehuevi, had come to Banning from the reservation at Twentynine Palms to work the fruit harvest, and they made camp at the ranch.

Willie Boy wanted to take in marriage William Mike's sixteen-year-old daughter Carlota (described variously by local whites as Isoleta, Neeta, Lolita, and Mabel),[15] but William Mike had refused. That night Willie Boy took a rifle from the Gilman storehouse and approached William Mike for Carlota's hand. Accounts vary about William Mike's death, from Willie Boy murdering the old man while he slept to the two men arguing and William Mike subsequently being killed in a struggle over the rifle.

Willie Boy threatened to kill the rest of the family if Carlota did not go with him, and her mother, Maria, urged her to go. Willie and Carlota headed out toward the desert on foot. Maria and her family, fearful of Willie Boy's vengeance and possible return, did not notify local Indian and white police authorities until 9:00 A.M. the next morning. A white posse, which at various times included among its numbers Joe Toutain, Charlie Reche, and the de Crevecoeur brothers Ben and Wal, set out after the couple.

The posse was assisted by two primary Indian trackers, John Hyde, a Yaqui, and Segundo Chino, a Chemehuevi, who had been friends of the Mike/Boniface family. Initially, some papers called the fugitive Billy Boy, an error corrected early, only to be reintroduced later by Madison when he joined the chase. From the beginning Willie Boy was misidentified as Paiute; a later correction describing him as Chemehuevi was not pursued in the local press and eventually became lost.[16]

Willie Boy and Carlota abandoned roads and trails, making their way north of Banning into the Morongo hills. The posse claimed to have pressed them hard, even to have heard the young woman whimpering at night in the distance ahead. But despite this alleged proximity, the posse could not close the distance and effect the capture. The trackers Hyde and Chino, who were in advance of the posse, pointed out the signs that Carlota was struggling, stumbling; that Willie Boy was prodding her with his rifle, beating her, urging her on. They discerned the signs that he was 25 "having his way with her" (the euphemism for rape). All those activities were supposedly revealed in signs on rock and sand, activities in which Willie Boy and Carlota could engage despite being hard-pressed by their pursuers!

On the morning of September 30, Charlie Reche was the first posseman reported to have come upon the body of Carlota on a boulder in an area known as The Pipes. What the local press meant, of course, was that Reche was the first white to find her corpse. Only one newspaper correctly observed that Hyde had been the one to find her.[17] But Reche got the credit, and Willie Boy got the blame. The posse returned to Banning with Carlota's body, and the townspeople were outraged.

The press immediately dubbed Willie Boy a double murderer, and officials printed wanted posters charging Willie Boy with the murder of "Old Mike" and his daughter (see fig. 1). As a double murderer, Willie Boy became a certifiable villain. Whites initially may have seen his kidnapping of a young woman and killing of his would-be father-in-law as a variation on the Romeo and Juliet theme, but no longer. Willie Boy was evil, and he must be made to pay the full price for his crimes. But if Willie Boy had killed Carlota, why

Arrest for Double Murder

San Bernardino, Cal., Oct. 5, 1909

Willie Boy

A Chimehuevis Indian. 26 years old, about 5 feet, 10 inches in height; slim built, walks and stands erect; yellowish complexion, sunken cheeks; high cheek bones; talks good English with a drawl; has a scar under chin where he has been shot and some teeth gone. For years lived about Victorville, with a halfbreed American woman with two children, a girl of 10 and a boy of 2 years. She left him because he had beaten her, and returned to Victorville. His people living among the Kingston mountains, along the Nevada state line. He killed Mike Boniface, at Banning on the night of Sunday, September 26, and Ioleta Boniface, at The Pipes, in San Bernardino county, September 30.

An Indian filling the description of Willie Boy was seen cooking a rabbit between Goffs Station and Manvel on Sunday evening, October 3rd. When he saw the approaching parties he ran away. This might have been Willie Boy as his mother was at Vanderbilt a short time ago. J. C. RALPHS, Sheriff.

Found dead Oct. 15-09.

Fig. 1. Willie Boy wanted poster, 1909 (Courtesy of Special Collections, Rivera Library, University of California, Riverside)

did he not flee? Reports abounded that he had gone to seek refuge with relatives at Twentynine Palms. Sheriff John C. Ralphs thus had them rounded up and brought to Banning attempting to deny Willie Boy sanctuary.

The Hunt for Willie Boy

The posse refitted and returned to the pursuit. On October 7, one week after Isoleta's body had been found and less than ten miles from that site, five possemen approached Bullion, later renamed Ruby Mountain. Hyde was in the lead as primary tracker, followed by Chino. The whites consisted of Reche, Wal de Crevecoeur, and Joe Knowlin. Hyde saw tracks that caused him to dismount and call the others to him. They too, dismounted to examine the signs, leaving the horses in the open while they joined Hyde to search among the rocks.

At that time Willie Boy ambushed them, shooting down three horses, wounding another, and scaring one away. During Willie Boy's shooting, one round hit Reche. The bullet splintered upon striking the handcuffs Reche carried on his hip (see fig. 2), and a fragment tore downward, causing a deep wound through hip and thigh. Reche lay sprawled on the ground, seriously wounded, and fully exposed to Willie Boy's rifle only thirty yards away.

During the encounter, words were exchanged between Willie Boy and the posse, including, allegedly, that Willie Boy wanted to shoot only Indians, not whites. Chino crawled around to get a better shot and fired several rounds toward the rock fort Willie Boy had erected. Meanwhile, Hyde ran to get word that Reche needed a doctor, which would mean a trip of thirty-five miles to a base camp followed by an additional journey back to Banning.

The posse waited until dark to move Reche, afraid of coming under Willie Boy's rifle fire. The deputy later reported that they awaited moonrise.[18] But his

Fig. 2. Posseman during Willie Boy manhunt wearing handcuffs on hip, 1909 (Courtesy of L. Burr Belden Collection in the Archives at the A. K. Smiley Public Library)

memory played him false, since there was no moon that night,[19] and darkness became the cover. As they were pulling out, with Reche stretched across the recaptured horse, Willie Boy fired his rifle again.

When the posse arrived at Banning, the whites were loathe to mention this last shot. Clara True, the Indian agent, thought that Willie Boy was dead; either he had committed suicide, which had been Chino's suspicion, or he had died from some wound Chino may have inflicted. For the press, however, such stories would have killed further interest in the case, so the Indian version, if reported at all, was included after what journalists call the skip, a concluding column inside the newspaper, frequently in smaller print.

The posse made no vigorous effort to refit this time. They and Willie Boy had pursued one another across nearly six hundred miles of desert, and the possemen were tired. Willie Boy had traversed that distance on foot, sometimes running very fast, averaging fifty miles a day, carrying a rifle and in the heat. On some days the temperature must have been close to 100 degrees. Hyde's run for help for Reche was impressive; Willie Boy had done much more, showing the endurance not simply of a marathon runner but of an athlete of extraordinary conditioning and abilities. The chase had been particularly hard, even for white men accustomed to the toughness of desert pursuit. To return to it, especially if the quarry was dead, could only have seemed a disagreeable anticlimax.

So the local press began to motivate the men. President Taft was going to visit San Bernardino, Redlands, and Riverside as part of a western swing of a national trip to buoy his presidential image. What if Willie Boy were not apprehended by then? Would the outlaw try to kill the president? Getting Willie Boy would be an act of national defense and a point of national pride.

Moreover, Willie Boy had a reputation for conflict with the law. The sheriff of San Bernardino County found that Willie Boy had served a ninety-day jail sentence in 1906, having been brought in from Victorville on a charge of disturbing the peace.[20] But such a charge, especially against an Indian, could have been for a petty reason. In March 1905, for example, the San Bernardino County jail held 83 prisoners for offenses ranging "from bicycle theft to murder"; a year later, during the month of August, 111 prisoners had been incarcerated, "of whom two [were] charged with murder, three with assault to commit murder, the other offenses ranging down to evading railway fare."[21]

On October 12, 1909, as if to commemorate the seventeenth anniversary of the first national Columbus Day, the *San Bernardino Daily Sun* made an astonishing discovery about Willie Boy that it announced with headlines: "Temperance Lesson in Blood, Drink Fest Is Cause of All the Trouble Brought on by Fugitive Indian." The source of the story was Ben de Crevecoeur. Although Willie Boy was from Twentynine Palms, de Crevecoeur's story appealed to the reputation for drunkenness among the Morongo Indians that was prevalent with local whites.

De Crevecoeur, a constable assisting Clara True, who was herself intolerant of anyone giving alcohol to Indians, allegedly discovered that a "white youth" who worked on the Gilman Ranch had purchased liquor in San Bernardino the Saturday before the violence began. The boy's mother had found and confiscated the cache but, after much pleading, had returned to him two bottles of whiskey and one of beer.

The youth then took them and hid them in the bunkhouse where he and Willie Boy were staying. De Crevecoeur concluded that Willie Boy had found the bottles and drunk their contents. It was the firewater that gave Willie Boy the "courage" to attack William Mike and steal his daughter. Other newspapers picked up the story and used it to fuel public outrage over Willie Boy's continued freedom.[22]

De Crevecoeur's tale struck home with Clara True. Her zeal in attacking bootleggers who sold whiskey to

30

Indians was of such ardor that her superior urged her to back off for her own safety.[23] But she persisted. In New York, at the Lake Mohonk Conference of the Friends of the Indian, a year earlier, she had proudly told the assembly that the Mission Indians under her care were less drunken than in earlier times. "The difference lay in the fact that the whiskey peddler was afraid to ply his trade this year because the San Bernardino jail was full of their kind *under sentence.* The *people* demanded the execution of the law [prohibiting sale of intoxicants to Indians] and it was forthcoming."[24] Clara True became indignant upon hearing that a white man had supplied Willie Boy with liquor.

De Crevecoeur did not identify the alleged white male. But now the story was complete. Demon drink had unleashed Willie Boy's lust and permitted him to act upon his base impulses. Alcohol had effectively uncorked the evil that lurked inside him. Earlier reports that he had been hard working, well respected, and not given to drink could now be easily forgotten. Resolving the Willie Boy chase then became an affirmation by whites of their need to protect themselves against drunken Indians. So the posse rode again, this time accompanied by a reporter from Los Angeles for the *Record,* Randolph Madison, to record the men's deeds in photographs and words.

As if to reinforce the posse's determination and to justify continuing the manhunt, the press reported rumors of Indian revolt to support Willie Boy, a plan to wage war under his leadership and drive the whites out. Indian agents in Southern California and Arizona had supposedly telegraphed the commissioner of Indian Affairs, warning of an impending outbreak of Paiutes and Chemehuevis; in turn these federal agents had been put on alert to communicate immediately any suspicious behavior to Washington, D.C.[25]

On October 15 the posse found Willie Boy at the ambush site. Ben de Crevecoeur received credit for the discovery, but it seems strange that Chino and other Indians had gone from trackers to trailers for this event. Willie Boy had removed his shoe, placed the rifle against his chest, and squeezed the trigger with his toe. That had been a week earlier, the last shot he fired as the posse had taken Reche out. In the interim his body had become bloated and badly decomposed. Someone suggested burning it, and so it was done. All that effort had been expended to find a man who had already denied his pursuers the satisfaction of white justice.

Through this last posse Madison laid the groundwork for Willie Boy's future incorporation into the mythic West. Madison was born and educated in the East, was related to President James Madison and to the Randolph family of Virginia, and was an excellent horseman. He had come to Los Angeles to work as a journalist and eventually was sent to the desert to join the chase. Although he thought de Crevecoeur a superior rider and tracker, he generally felt distaste for the white possemen, and so Madison spread his blanket among the Indian trackers for their warmth and company.[26]

It was Madison — with Indian assistance, abetted by de Crevecoeur because he later retold the episode — who learned of an astonishing accomplishment by the young woman. "Near the spot where they found the body of . . . Isoleta [Carlota] . . . were strange hieroglyphics marked on a limestone formation with a piece of harder stone. Segundo Chino and Jack Hyde . . . interpreted them as follows: 'My heart is gone. I soon will be dead.'"[27] This message was indeed amazing for someone whose native language had no written form! But stories of rape and violence, coupled with Carlota's/Isoleta's supposed fears and unwillingness to be with Willie Boy, sold newspapers.

The posse found over twenty pounds of supplies around Willie Boy's body, as Madison reported, including twenty pounds of flour, some rice and beans, along with a can each of tomatoes and condensed milk.[28] Madison filed some stories locally with the *San Bernardino Daily Sun* and the *Redlands Daily Facts* in addition to his own Los Angeles newspaper, the *Record*. He issued stories through the Newspaper Enterprise Association, and his work appeared regionally and in some national papers.

Madison wrote against the grain of his times by trying to relate his view of Willie Boy to the Indian's supposed Paiute culture. In his most sympathetic story, headlined "He Wanted Her—He Took Her—But He Couldn't Be a Piute [*sic*] in the White Man's Country," Madison attributed the entire episode to "the blood of his fathers calling him," to Willie Boy's reversion to savagery and to Indian custom. For Madison, burning Willie Boy's body was Indian ceremonial cremation, a Paiute funeral.[29]

Madison derived these insights from his conversations with de Crevecoeur, Chino, and Hyde. Madison, the easterner, did not find it an odd custom that an Indian culture in the exotic West would initiate marriage and future family life by the groom's murdering his prospective father-in-law and then kidnapping his intended bride. Madison's confidence in these various alleged Paiute customs had greatest impact, however, not in his own day but later, on fellow journalist Harry Lawton. Attributing false customs to Indians to explain their behavior simply reconfirmed reasons to hate them.

To avoid disappointing their readers at the time, the major printed stories focused on the posse's hard work in supposedly wearing Willie Boy down to his last bullet at Ruby Mountain, driving him to the desperation of suicide. What before had been the site of Willie Boy's ambush and further defiance of white authority became instead, with the discovery of his body, the scene of his "last stand." The reporting in the *Los Angeles Herald* on October 17, exemplifies the power of that journalistic transformation in a single, lengthy sentence:

> Willie Boy is dead, and with his death is ended the meteoric career of probably the most famous Indian renegade of late years, whose trail was blazed by two of the most cruel murders in the criminal annals of the two counties in which they occurred and by the most thrilling manhunt in the history of the great dreary desert, in the desolate midst of which, huddled in his lonely rock protected garrison, the desperate Piute [*sic*] murderer, broken in spirit by the hardships of the long chase and weak from the exposure and hunger, cheated his pursuers from their ambition of capture by using his last cartridge to end the life sought by a horde of officers whom, he thought would, in a few hours, close in on him.

The Hunt for Willie Boy

Thus the chase, newspapers assured their readers, had been worth the effort after all. The story soon faded from the press and passed into local Southern California lore, without, however, the Los Angeles notion that the posses had been cheated out of anything.

Yet, whether they troubled the sensibilities of locals or not, questions had been raised by the Willie Boy episode that persisted. If Willie Boy had been drunk, how did he manage to kill a man, kidnap his daughter, evade her family, and flee? Did he not need to sleep it off somewhere, sometime? Why did it take so long for word of his drinking to surface? How had William Mike died: by murder or by accident? How could a man on foot outrun a posse on horses? If Willie Boy loved Carlota, why would he kill her? Was not his feeling for her the reason for his actions? Why would he return to the scene of his crime if he knew that she was already dead? Since Willie Boy was not out of food at Ruby Mountain, why should we think that he was out of ammunition? And why did Indian trackers Chino and Hyde incite the white posse to greater anger against Willie Boy? Why did Chino and Hyde gamble that their fueling white hatred toward Willie Boy would not be directed against other Indians as well? This question becomes more urgent within the context of local Indian-white relations over Morongo land. Were Chino and Hyde using whites just as whites used them? Most of these questions, however, were not raised as the story was retold over the years; they are the basis, however, for seeing how Indian-hating is perpetuated.

3

The White Man's Willie Boy in Non?-Fiction

The Willie Boy story entered local lore as a fable about Indian behavior. It had all the necessary ingredients to become part of the American frontier myth, but it needed an effective agent to bring it to a wider audience; Harry Lawton became that agent. Originally, the most direct moral of the Willie Boy story was a reiteration of the old warning against Indians' using alcohol—it transformed them into "bad" Indians. An unholy coupling of alcohol and lust produced untoward violence and murder. The tale thus affirmed the virtues of white law enforcement in which the Indian antagonist caricatured evil to underscore further the goodness of those doing right; the tale exemplified Indian-hating.

Getting at the essential story—determining what really happened and then assessing meaning—became progressively more difficult. By the third time it appeared in print, in 1939, Tom Hughes, a recorder of local lore, noted that earlier accounts of Willie Boy's having had prior Indian wives or of having caused the disappearance of a white prospector "seem to have been fastened upon him out of pure generosity."[1]

As it evolved, the story became multilayered, like the initial reporting altered by rewrite men, until it gathered levels of encrusted half-truths and falsehoods of such thickness that sorting out the real from the unreal became a formidable task—provided, of course, one wanted to bother with such sorting at all. When Lawton took up the task twenty years after Hughes, he thought that fifty years of storytelling "has so legendized it that the truth becomes impossible to ferret out."[2]

THE TALE AND THE TELLERS

Over the years the story was told and retold orally. Nina Howard Paul [Shumway] used it as a plot complication in her 1926 fictional story "The Purple Boundary." Willie Boy became "Squint" Lopez, "a half-loco 'breed' . . . who dragged a girl from the reservation away into these hills, murdered her and worse."[3] The rape image held sufficient horror for whites that it could be considered worse than death itself.

When Nina Paul Shumway wrote her nonfiction version of the story, she drew heavily on Ben de Crevecoeur's version as told to a third party. In her account Willie Boy had shared "a suitcase full of liquor" with his white friend before beginning his rampage. In her view, Willie Boy had shot Carlota/Isoleta in the back, when she staggered against a rock, because she had become a drag slowing his flight.[4] In this aspect Shumway repeated the thinking of the first reporters; Willie Boy, having satisfied himself sexually at her expense, cruelly murdered the girl when she became an impediment to his escape.

The earliest retellings drew upon the recollections of several white possemen. But the accounts given by Ben de Crevecoeur and Charlie Reche proved the most popular with locals and occasional visiting journalists. Some of the embellishments were astonishing. Using Ben de Crevecoeur and Reche, Willard S. Wood added that, in tracking Willie Boy and Carlota/Isoleta, the posse "on a smooth bit of wind-blown sand found where the girl had scrawled in Piute [*sic*] signs 'He is going to kill me.' "[5]

Following the ambush, the posse would not attempt Reche's rescue "until moonrise which was not due til two in the morning." And when they heard the "single muffled shot," they talked about it and decided: "That's the end of Willie Boy."[6] The nonexistent moonrise had become part of the telling. So too had the white claim to have known from the moment of Willie Boy's last shot from his ambush site that the chase was done. That sentiment helps explain the subsequent delay in pursuit.

Carlota's written message became a minor theme in much of the retelling. In his 1939 account, drawn again from the primary tellers, Tom Hughes wrote, "The pursuers saw where the girl had left writings in the sand, but they were in Chemuhuevi [*sic*], and no one in the posse could read their message."[7]

Two years later, James Carling, relying almost exclusively on Ben de Crevecoeur, elaborated on the message. He drew it as an illustration (see fig. 3), and Ben told him that it had been scrawled in the mud and later translated by Jim Pine from the Twentynine Palms Reservation. It supposedly read, "My heart is almost gone. . . . I will be dead soon."[8] As can be seen from the drawing, all of this is nonsense— California Indians did not have a written language, and the young woman was illiterate[9]—but its purpose in the story is clear: Carlota was taken against her will and then murdered by Willie Boy.

The Carling version may have been Ben de Crevecoeur's most outrageous retelling of the tale, what with changing the liquor story, pushing the written message, and detailing the villainy of Willie Boy that years earlier Hughes cautioned had been attached to the Indian out of "pure generosity." Although de Crevecoeur "was as windy as a cow on green pasture,"[10] as one local phrased it, or "a likeable blowhard," in the words of Harry Lawton,[11] de Crevecoeur's stories continued to circulate uncritically (see Appendix, item no. 2 and several others).

Subsequent writers repeated the refrains that Ben de Crevecoeur and Reche had established. With de Crevecoeur's obvious knack for storytelling—inserting himself into events in the chase in which he had not directly participated[12]—the tale centered on the white posse and the pursuit, with all the Indians except the villain and victims receding into deep shadow. And

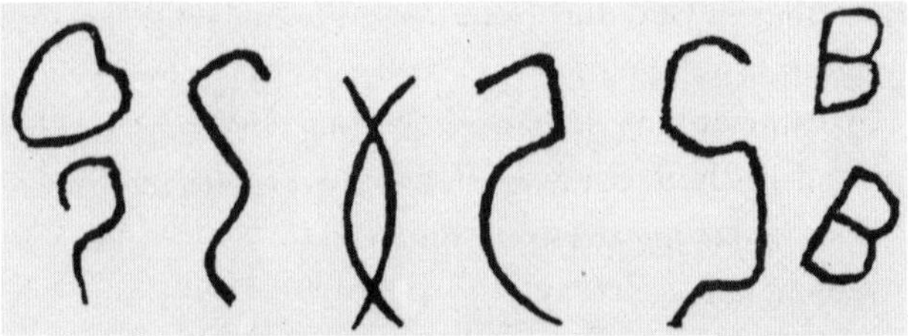

Fig. 3. Message allegedly written by Carlota/Isoleta Mike during flight. The message was translated by Indian Jim Pine as, "My heart is almost gone . . . I will be dead soon." (From a story by James L. Carling, *Desert Magazine* [November 1941]:6.)

the story remained compact. Willie Boy drank half a suitcase full of liquor, murdered William Mike in his sleep, took the girl (in several instances her age was reduced to fourteen) against her will, sexually and physically abused her, finally murdered her, then ran off across the desert. For unknown reasons he returned to the scene of his crime against her. Surprised by lawmen, he ambushed the posse and, fearing he would be taken, killed himself.

Reche's handcuffs became the symbol of white victory, for although he never got to put them on Willie Boy, they had saved his life and somehow forced Willie Boy to forfeit his own. But none of these accounts acknowledged what the *Los Angeles Herald* had observed at the time: Willie Boy denied the posse its objective. Willie Boy, not the posse, chose his death; Willie boy cheated his white pursuers, but no local dared to say it.[13]

In the last printed version before Harry Lawton's, journalist John Q. Copeland raised some new points. He had interviewed surviving possemen Reche and Joe Toutain, and he wrote of a rivalry between the two primary storytellers de Crevecoeur and Reche, a rivalry rooted in their county affiliations as possemen. De Crevecoeur represented Riverside County law enforcement, whereas Reche was a deputy commissioned by the sheriff of San Bernardino County. When de Crevecoeur's men and Reche's joined forces, Reche accused de Crevecoeur of "hogging headlines." After finding the girl's corpse and returning it to Banning, Reche chose his own "personal posse" to go after Willie Boy, a group limited to de Crevecoeur's brother Wal, Joe Toutain, Joe Knowlin, and the Indian trackers Segundo Chino and John Hyde. Reche did not invite Ben de Crevecoeur.

This "personal posse" was the group ambushed at Ruby Mountain. Reche mistakenly remembered that he had been shot from his saddle, and he now had the whole posse mounted for the shootout instead of on the ground moving among the rocks as they had been. And Toutain avowed that after hearing Willie Boy's last shot, he would not ride again if Reche believed the Indian dead. Thus de Crevecoeur participated in the last posse and brought the story to an end that Reche thought should have belonged to himself.[14]

Besides de Crevecoeur's use of the Willie Boy episode to advance his job aspirations, the political side of the chase also became a factor in the lives of others. Sheriff John Ralphs of San Bernardino County was convinced by a united Board of Supervisors of the "absolute necessity of disposing of the murderous" Willie Boy.[15] In later years Ralphs's career highlights always included the posse and Willie Boy. An obituary account in the *San Bernardino Sun* referred to Ralphs's life as a page "out of the Old West" largely because of the Willie Boy episode.

That a successful resolution of the Willie Boy affair proved vital to the reelection interests of Frank Wilson can be seen in the jockeying for position in the 1910 Riverside County sheriff's campaign. P. M. Coburn, former sheriff, declared his candidacy in December 1909. The *Riverside Morning Mission* pointedly observed that Coburn was a "come on, boys" rather than a "go on, boys" man, a dig at Wilson's sporadic leadership of his posse.[16] By March 1910, Wilson, out hustling votes, came to Banning where he spent the day getting petitions signed by supporters—a large number of whom were men who had participated in the Willie Boy chase.[17]

HARRY LAWTON AND THE MYTHIC WEST

When Harry Lawton retold the tale, he brought it explicitly into the mythology of the West. "When the Willie Boy manhunt began on September 26, 1909, the Western frontier was already dead. Its demise dated back at least two decades, possibly longer. Yet the Wild West was revived for one last florid curtain call by the Willie Boy affair."[18]

Intentionally or not, Lawton identified the saga with America's most powerful myth—the advance of "civilization" westward—and its termination with the supposed closing of the frontier. The Willie Boy episode then became both a nostalgic lament for the passing of the West (one last florid curtain call) and an example of how the West had been won.

As an example of the frontier myth, the story had to assume a certain telling that would necessarily convey the white attitude without concern for expressing an Indian view. The multiple posses embodied the spirit of the city, with its law and order spreading across and pacifying the wilderness. The possemen represented Western goodness, "civilization," taming what was untamable in the West, the "savage" Indian. From earliest American literary writing the Indian had been portrayed as "a set of contradictions: noble and ignoble, pitied and praised, censured and celebrated."[19]

Lawton repeats that formula. First he praises the Indian: "Whatever one may think of Willie Boy, his feat [of endurance] commands respect." But in his epigraph, Lawton gives his readers a story from *Pioneering the West* that tells of an Indian "buck" getting a wife by shooting her father to death in his sleep.[20] Lawton's epigraph prefigures his tale: Willie Boy begins his rampage by the premeditated, senseless slaying of a sleeping William Mike. Lawton chose the epigraph to establish "a feeling in the reader's mind that W[illie] B[oy] may be carrying out an old custom."[21] Both praised and condemned, Willie Boy is elevated by Lawton to the status of worthy opponent for his posse.

Lawton expanded the story's scope on the basis of his more extensive research into the press coverage of the time. Lawton claimed that "legend and an American President have robbed Willie Boy of his name. He was not Willie Boy. . . . all knew him as Billy Boy." The press, however, according to Lawton, had changed his name in deference to the visit from President Taft, whose nickname was Billy Boy. Lawton decided to allow the legend of Willie Boy to continue this alteration of his name.[22] As we have already seen, however, Willie Boy was his name, and Billie or Billy Boy the error.[23]

Lawton chose to call the young woman Lolita,[24] certainly a variant used in some accounts, but also a name that suggested Vladimir Nabokov's *Lolita* (1955), a novel about the relationship between "a desperate pervert and a wretched child,"[25] a story of an older man's obsession with a twelve-year-old, sexually awakening nymphet. With each mention of her name, this symbolism of Lolita further reinforced Willie Boy's depravity.[26]

Ethnographically, Lawton identified the young Indian woman and her family as Chemehuevi and Willie Boy as Paiute.[27] In calling Willie Boy a Paiute, Lawton chose to discount conflicting press accounts and to "confirm" the Indian custom stories of Randolph Madison. Lawton reinforced his decision because Joe Toutain thought that Willie Boy came from Nevada.[28] In making his choice, Lawton went against the recommendation of his publisher, Horace Parker, who correctly thought that the Boniface/Mike family and Willie Boy were all Chemehuevis.[29]

Lawton wove elements of Paiute ethnography into various points of his imaginary dialogue and the thoughts he gave to the two Indians in their flight. In this manner Lawton thought to show an Indian side to the story. However, within the shape of the frontier myth—which has Indian-hating as an essential component—the Indian side could not explain anything different from the white view. An Indian side could only elaborate upon or confirm that view. Since the primary culture to which Willie Boy belonged was Chemehuevi, as some of the local press at the time and as Lawton's publisher thought, then Lawton had Willie Boy following the wrong Indian customs.

Lawton began with the liquor episode but handled it differently. "Fictional names have been substituted for the real names of two persons in the book, Clem Newcombe and Bill Holden," he told his readers. "How I met Holden—whose identity Ben de Crevecouer [sic] kept secret—and persuaded him to tell his story might make a fascinating yarn in itself."[30] Allegedly, these two men bought the whiskey in San Bernardino and Holden hid a partially consumed bottle in the bunkhouse on the Gilman Ranch, where Willie Boy later found and drank it.[31]

45

Once Lawton had Willie Boy consume the liquor, the story followed the conventional path, with detailed elaborations of individual events and re-created scenes invested with invented dialogue. Willie Boy killed "Old Mike" as he lay sleeping and took the "girl" by force. Charlie Reche found her body where Willie Boy had let her fall; Willie Boy ran off into the desert. Lawton noted that the coroner had not performed a medical examination of the young woman's corpse and so could neither confirm nor deny charges of sexual assault.[32] By rejecting the coroner's report in the matter of her death, however, and by presenting Willie Boy's conviction of her murder in the press, Lawton too made Willie Boy a double murderer after whatever happened at The Pipes.[33]

In giving assent to Willie Boy's alleged murder of the young woman, Lawton again went against the thinking of his publisher, Horace Parker. Parker believed that she had been killed by someone other than Willie Boy, probably a posseman.[34] While researching the story, Lawton had wondered, too, whether an Indian tracker might have fired the shot that killed Isoleta.[35] These contradictory thoughts, however, did not enter his final version of the story.

Lawton portrayed Willie Boy's flight to Twentynine Palms from The Pipes as a desperate search for another weapon and food, both of which are denied to him by a toothless, mocking old Indian woman. An enraged Willie Boy then beats her, further reinforcing the image of Willie Boy the savage. Lawton offered no reason for Willie Boy's return to the vicinity of The Pipes. At Ruby Mountain, the renamed Bullion Mountain, Willie Boy shoots the horses out from under the possemen, ignoring Reche's and Hyde's original account that they were dismounted when ambushed. Following Reche's misrecollection, Lawton has the possemen wait until the nonexistent moonrise to remove their wounded comrade. In this version, Reche knew that the single shot they heard signaled Willie Boy's suicide.[36]

Lawton extended his version to include Randolph Madison's coverage of the last posse's return to Ruby Mountain. Lawton appreciated Madison's journalism, his willingness to ride with the posse, and his view of the manhunt as a tragedy accompanying the closing of the frontier. Madison had photographed as well as written about the men, and Lawton obtained an old collection of Madison's photographs.

Lawton used Madison's photographs extensively to illustrate his story, which he dedicated to posse member "Joe Toutain the first to ride, the last to go." Lawton made no mention of any rivalry between Reche and de Crevecoeur,[37] nor did he question de Crevecoeur's stories. Lawton simply omitted de Crevecoeur's version of the written message, concluding that the "Indian writing is probably Ben's hokum."[38] Lawton's printed book differed sharply from his initial venture, which contained endnotes discussing points of disagreement and elaborating on the text. At some point Lawton changed his approach. "I'm not going to destroy the facts to achieve my ends," he tried to reassure his publisher Parker, "but they do have a habit of slyly intruding themselves at the exact points in the narrative when they shouldn't."[39] Finally, the dramatic narrative smoothed away the contradictions and eliminated the conflicting accounts of a scholarly narrative.[40]

Lawton grafted his version of the Willie Boy story to the literary landscape of the West and earned important recognition for his book. Some of the biggest names in literary and historical writing endorsed it: historian J. Frank Dobie, Western writers Ferol Egan and William Hogan, desert bibliographer E. I. Edwards, columnists Ed Ainsworth and John Connell, and esteemed librarian, bibliographer, and historian Lawrence Clark Powell.[41] In 1960 Lawton won the James D. Phelan Award for nonfiction for *Willie Boy: A Desert Manhunt*, producing thereby the oxymoron of a "nonfiction novel."

Not everyone expressed enthusiasm for the book. Lawton's publisher, Horace Parker, sought out local newspaperman Frank Moore and presented his long-standing criticisms. Moore, along with his brother, wrote a popular column entitled "A Grain of Salt" for their newspaper the *Redlands Daily Facts*. The Moores decided to print Parker's major disagreement, namely, that a posseman, not Willie Boy, had killed the girl, probably accidentally.[42] Parker's surprising version did not draw much attention, and he lamented later within his family that he regretted not having written the story of Willie Boy himself.[43]

LAWTON AND THE CAHUILLA

Lawton had talked with some Indians, mainly Cahuilla, from the Morongo Reservation and, in the final chapter of his novel, described an Indian version of the legend.

> The Indians also have their version of the legend. They scoff at reports that Willie Boy's body was burned on the ridge at Ruby Mountain. He escaped into Mexico, where he married and had many children. He passed away with tuberculosis in a Nevada sanitorium in 1933. Some insist they heard the story of his escape from his own lips. . . .
>
> The glamor of Willie Boy's fictitious uprising still clings to his name. Among the Desert and Pass Indians there are aging tribesmen who feel he represented something, stood for some romantic cause, although they scratch their heads and lapse into silence if asked to explain.[44]

This two-paragraph description of an "Indian version" did not include material from the family members of either group directly involved. It was a generic account, and again, within the framework of the history of the West, it could explain nothing contrary to the white view. It did, however, show Lawton as trying to be sensitive to Paiute and Cahuilla Indians. Jane Penn, Cahuilla elder and historian of the predominantly Cahuilla Morongo Reservation, told Lawton that he had "written the book for Indians, because it is written as the Indians would tell it, only in a different language. . . . We are fortunate that you were the one to write about Willie Boy as you have, as long as I've known you, made every effort to understand my people."[45]

While making *Tell Them Willie Boy Is Here,* director Abraham Lincoln Polonsky was urged by Lawton to do some filming on the Morongo Reservation, bringing much-needed employment to some reservation residents. Lawton and Polonsky donated wanted posters and film artifacts to the Malki Museum on the reservation so that the Cahuilla could create a display on the Willie Boy episode.

Thus the Cahuilla, through the book and the film, just like Jane Penn suggested, came to identify with Willie Boy, the alleged Paiute. So strong did that identification become that one observer remarked that they "have accepted the renegade as one of their own."[46] Lawton's interest in the Morongo Reservation over the years, combined with the Cahuilla interest in Willie Boy, led in 1976 to the Cahuilla's reissuing *Willie Boy: A Desert Manhunt* under the auspices of the Malki Museum Press.[47]

Lawton's book, which included a description of finding Willie Boy's cremation site, inspired local law enforcement officials to erect a monument to their accomplishments at the place where Willie Boy's body had been found and burned. The original, wire-framed tribute, holding a placard describing the events and affixed to a spike, was dedicated on October 9, 1966.

According to the *San Bernardino Sheriff's Association Newsletter,* "The Sheriffs Rangers fenced off and marked the spot . . . where 'Willie Boy, the Mad Dog of the Morongos,' made his last defiant stand against the pursuing arm of the law. This historical landmark was not placed as a shrine to an outlaw, but as a single mark on a once wild and savage land which is quickly diminishing under the consuming, expanding population explosion."[48]

Both Lawton and Jane Penn attended the ceremony. Penn was the only Indian present, representing the contribution of Indian trackers from Morongo to the manhunt.[49] It was not recorded whether anyone noted the irony of erecting a monument to law-and-order on the site of a suicide. In keeping with the persistent unruliness of some corners of the West, however, the marker was repeatedly vandalized over the years until a new, bronze plaque was embedded in concrete on the site in 1987. It yet remains in place (see fig. 4).

By weaving Cahuilla observations on Willie Boy into his text, Lawton set the stage for ongoing Cahuilla commitment to his version of the story. The Cahuilla interest, however well intended, drew them unwittingly into the vortex of the metaphysics of Indian-hating. The Cahuilla are not Paiute, nor are they Chemehuevi. Cahuilla endorsement of Lawton's

Fig. 4. The monument to law enforcement at the Willie Boy suicide site (Photo by Tom Morr)

novel and their subsequent involvement in the film have meant conferring a legitimacy to this version of the story that helped to embed it in popular culture.

The Cahuilla were not the only Indians praising Lawton's Willie Boy. In mid-1991, a Navajo-Mexican writer reviewing books in *News from Native California* pronounced Lawton's book "a classic in Western writing," one that has withstood the test of time. He praised it and the film made from it as far more accurate than most work on Indians.[50]

THE TALE SINCE LAWTON

The Willie Boy story continues to be retold, but the published versions since 1960, as the Appendix shows, have almost all been based upon Lawton's fictional account. By the mid-1980s one writer observed that "each year the story is told, in various forms, in local desert newspapers. It's as though the chase continues in the deserts surrounding Ruby Mountain."[51]

Over the years, however, an important shift has occurred in where the story is presented. In 1963 W. Douglas Lansford, who later wrote a popular biography of famed Mexican revolutionary leader General

Francisco "Pancho" Villa, published his account of Willie Boy in a sleazy men's magazine in which his story did not get highlighted on the cover. Lansford's version lost title billing to such provocative entries as "Town That Sex Built!" "Berlin Crashout!" and "Stag Parties, U.S.A."[52]

A quarter of a century later in 1989, Western writer Harold L. Edwards published his rendition in the glossy history magazine *The Californians*. Edwards's version was accompanied by a meditative poem composed by poet Dick Barnes inspired by Barnes's reading of Lawton's book.[53]

Willie Boy's story has stirred activity beyond the written word. Twenty-five years after the monument had been dedicated at Willie Boy's cremation site, myth as caricature has reached its apotheosis in the Sixth Annual Willie Boy Days and Festival held at Landers, near Twentynine Palms. A reenacting of the final posse ride, tributes to sheriffs old and new, a carnival, food booths, and special store sales belie the tragedy of a love story gone awry and a posse that never could catch its prey but by stalking a long-dead corpse. The celebration now falls on Mother's Day weekend.

Echoing the sentiments surrounding the dedication of the original monument, George Hertel, the 1991 ride organizer, claimed, "We're not trying to glorify him but the men who caught up with him."[54] Lawton's Willie Boy has helped this community promote itself by invoking its past. Some of the advertisements convey the spirit: a real estate company announces "We'll sell you a homestead or a piece of Willie's Place," a hardware store proclaims "He ain't hidin' here—Buy yer ropes, traps, bait and varmit catchin' supplies here," a liquor store advises "We're right smack in the middle o' Willie Boy's trail! Ya can't miss it," and one family-owned business says "[We] settled Landers after the posse chased Willie out but we're all going to celebrate Willie Boy Days."[55]

From a manhunt in 1909 to a celebration and sale eight decades later, the white man's Willie Boy continues to perpetuate Indian-hating but today in more subtle, less obvious ways. The Willie Boy story has grown in popularity, especially in the last thirty years, largely because of Lawton and the movie inspired by his book. We turn now to the image of Willie Boy in film.

4

The White Man's Willie Boy in Hollywood

In the late 1960s and early 1970s, American film critics began to talk of a "new" Indian movie, a *Cinéma Rouge,* which supposedly presented Native Americans in ways that went beyond traditional stereotypes. Abraham Lincoln Polonsky's *Tell Them Willie Boy Is Here* (Universal, 1969) was initially considered such a film.[1] But, as Indians and other observers noted, despite its obvious theme of Indian-white relations, the film generated much more news about the return of its director to filmmaking after a long absence forced by his blacklisting in the 1950s.[2] Why the initial positive thinking followed by disappointment? The answer lies partially in the structure of filmmaking and its relationship to a literary source and partially in the competing and conflicting messages sent out by this sophisticated movie. But there is a more fundamental bias working as well.

When a book is translated into film, the movie necessarily looks different from the original text because each medium is different, one depending upon mental images, the other upon visual. Moreover, the Willie Boy incident, by subject matter, belongs to the genre of the Western. Traditionally, Hollywood has depicted Indians in several ways, none of which have been concerned with presenting Indians as Indians, on their own cultural terms. Even well-intended efforts such as Kevin Costner's *Dances With Wolves* (Orion, 1990) are severely constrained by the metaphysics of Indian-hating.[3] Costner elevates the Sioux while reducing the Pawnee to marauding muggers. The stereotypical Hollywood Indians that have emerged over the past eighty years have been insults to all Native Americans.[4] Thus, when analyzing a film about Indians, we must keep in mind these two major limitations: the bias of Indian-hating and the constraints of filmmaking.

Of all the approaches to the Western film, the one we find most satisfying for our purpose is that of Jon Tuska. He classifies Westerns into three types, based upon function, calling them "the formulary Western, the romantic historical reconstruction (historical romance), and the historical reconstruction." Willie Boy belongs to the category of historical reconstruction containing a plot situation he calls the "Law Man" combined with the "Indian Story."[5]

Tuska sees the story structure of the romance, which has relevance for the Willie Boy film, as little changed from the days of classical antiquity. "The ancient Greeks divided romance into three stages," he writes. "The first, the *agon*, means a conflict of some sort. The second stage is the *pathos*, the life-and-death struggle. The third and final stage is the *anagnorisis*, the recognition. There is an optional middle term which, when present, proves pivotal in determining whether the story is merely formulary or a romantic historical reconstruction and this is the *sparagmos*, the mangling."[6]

In the historical reconstruction, to which category Willie Boy belongs, there is no necessary or assumed reason for the struggle, and the chief protagonist need not be a hero. It is up to this person to choose to act as a hero. Tuska's conceptualization, with his discussion of the *pathos*, the *anagnorisis*, and the *sparagmos*, permits us to approach Polonsky's *Tell Them Willie Boy Is Here* with both sensitivity to Polonsky's accomplishments and appreciation of the limits to which he and the genre are subject.

TELL THEM WILLIE BOY IS HERE

When Polonsky rewrote Lawton's story for the screen, he made significant changes, some of which adversely affected historical accuracy. We have traced these changes through three script versions (early, first, and final) and compare the written to the final filmed version.[7] Let us begin by summarizing the film. Polonsky composed his story around four main characters—two women and two men.

Polonsky chose to call the young Indian woman "Lola," perhaps for ease of pronunciation, since the other names, except Willie Boy, are a single syllable; he thus effectively neutralized the pejorative effect of the name Lolita. And Katherine Ross, who played Lola, did not look like a teenager. Polonsky called the white female Indian agent at the Morongo Reservation "Liz," short for Elizabeth Arnold. He described her as leggy and handsome, an anthropologist and an M.D., a woman who believed in the vote for women and a single sexual standard. Susan Clark played her.

The primary male characters were "Willie Boy," played by Robert Blake, who was to embody athletic grace and look like a "poker-faced, Paiute Indian"; and "Coop," portrayed by Robert Redford, the under-sheriff of Banning and son of a famous lawman and Indian hunter. Coop's father had been killed by a drunken mixed blood some time before the story begins. Of the minor characters, the most significant, in terms of setting the tone of the film, is "Ray," played by Barry Sullivan. Ray had fought Indians with Coop's father and constantly reminisces about the old days. "Me and your father," he tells Coop, "we killed a lot of Indians in our time. Good men. Real good scouts and hunters." But now, all has changed. Coop's father died, Ray says, back "when it was still good to live." Ray is a one-man Greek chorus lamenting the passing of the frontier.

Liquor initiates the action—not from a bottle found stashed in a bunkhouse but from a bottle Willie Boy purchased from a bootlegger ("blind pigger") on the Morongo Reservation at Banning. Afterward Willie Boy heads into town and drops into the pool hall for a game. He enters through swinging doors on which is printed a sign, barely visible in the final cut, "No Indians Allowed." On the table in the foreground are two glasses filled with beer, in front of two loafers. The men in the pool hall are supposed to react to Willie Boy because he is an Indian; instead, they hardly react at all. The entrance is more Blake playing a white rebel than an Indian confronting a white-imposed taboo. When a salesman offers to play anyone a game, even for a penny, Blake antes up. When the salesman tells him to get back to the reservation, Blake strikes him in the head with the butt of his cue, menaces the onlookers, and flees. As played, the scene portrays Willie Boy as a hothead, an impetuous young man with a proclivity for violence, an Indian who has already had enough whiskey to be trouble-some. Missing from the film is the dialogue Polonsky wrote into the scene showing the salesman's racism and building to the challenge, put-down, and assault.

Willie Boy returns to the ranch where he has previously arranged to meet Lola, in the orchard, at midnight. He stops by the bunkhouse and has a few more pulls from the bottle with his white bunkmate, then takes a blanket and heads for his rendezvous. He is unarmed.

A short time later, in the orchard, Willie Boy and Lola are naked, talking. Lola says that Dr. Arnold (Liz) wants her to become a teacher. Perhaps they can go to Nevada, where Lola can teach school and Willie Boy can have his own ranch. But Willie Boy is upset. Her father has rejected him and chased him with a gun. "I asked for you Indian way and white man's way," he declares, "and I'm no man to be kept waiting." He then pulls her to him on the ground. At that point the lovers are caught in flagrante delicto by her father and two brothers; in the ensuing struggle for the rifle, a clearly naked Willie Boy kills Old Mike, while Lola covers herself with her white dress.

Meanwhile, the relationship of Liz and Coop has been intercut with the tale of the Indian lovers, offering parallels and contrasts between white and Indian love, between "civilization" and "savagery." After arresting the "blind piggers" on the reservation on Liz's orders, Coop lets them go after dark because he wants to come back and spend the night with her. He is almost thwarted by Willie Boy's violence at the pool hall, but he tells the salesman to go to bed and fill out a complaint in the morning. When the salesman protests, Coop admonishes him by saying that if Willie Boy's intent had been to kill, the salesman would be dead. Thus Coop is able to return to the reservation— and Liz's quarters.

Liz says she does not want to let him in, but he succeeds anyway. Theirs is a relationship based upon lust, not love, and both parties have little use for one another outside the bed. He thinks that she wants him to tell her he loves her—well, he won't. She claims to see in him everything that is coarse and brutal; that is precisely what makes him exciting to her eastern-educated sensibilities. Coop says nastily that even though she is a doctor, she can look upon a man "in his natural state" only when he is a cadaver; she cannot look at Coop naked during their lovemaking. To underscore the point, we catch a glimpse of Liz naked under the sheet; Coop is always shown nearly fully clothed. The "savage" Willie Boy and Lola, naked in the orchard, contrast with the "civilized" whites, one naked and one partially clothed, in their bed.

For story convenience, Polonsky reduced the multiple posses to one and made of the main character, Redford's Coop, a composite of Toutain, Reche, the de Crevecoeurs, and others. The Indian trackers, played by Indians from the Morongo Reservation, become trailers behind the keen-eyed whites, Coop and Ray. The ambush at Ruby Mountain follows Lawton in that the posse is mounted, but it differs in that Lola is still alive and present. While Lola may have fled under duress initially, in the film she bonds to Willie Boy during their flight, becoming his wife. After the ambush, she and Willie Boy flee to Twentynine Palms, where they find what his relatives have left him: some money, a loaded revolver, and his father's "ghost shirt."

The "ghost shirt" symbolism, while powerful, may have been a reference to a historical event little known to film viewers. The Ghost Dance of the late nineteenth century, which culminated on December 29, 1890, in the massacre of 150 Sioux at Wounded Knee by U.S. army soldiers, signified the extreme limit of Indian resistance to white domination. This shirt should signal to the audience Willie Boy's willingness to fight to his death.[8]

Coop, meanwhile, had been diverted to Riverside to protect President William Howard Taft on his visit to the area. When he learns of the ambush and the wounding of Ray, Coop realizes his responsibility and blames himself for the cause of the trouble. This is his *sparagmos.* Coop tells Liz that had it not been for his lust for her, he would have done his job that night, he would have kept the "blind piggers" in jail and acted on the salesman's complaint by arresting Willie Boy. Since Coop's failure to act as a hero has brought on the trouble, he is the only one who can resolve it. Thus Coop must choose to return to the chase. When he and some possemen do reach Twentynine Palms, they find Willie Boy gone and Lola's corpse on the ground. This discovery provokes differing views of how she died, especially among the confused Indians. One man says Willie Boy killed her, another that she killed herself to free his flight. Now Coop is even firmer in his resolve and pursues Willie Boy with single-minded fury.

For dramatic intensity, Polonsky portrays the ending as a contest between Redford's Coop and Blake's Willie Boy, in which Blake dons his father's Ghost Dance shirt and confronts Redford menacingly. Coop shoots and kills Willie Boy (the *pathos*), only to discover that Willie Boy was out of ammunition. Coop wonders if Willie Boy knew Coop, at least in Polonsky's script, decides Willie Boy knew; it is part of Coop's *anagnorisis.* Willie Boy has forced the white man to kill him, and the magic of the Ghost Dance shirt, which was held to be impervious to white bullets, fails. Coop brings the body to the base of Ruby Mountain and has it burned. The flames and smoke of Willie Boy's funeral pyre fill the screen as the final scene fades.

The film has two characters who become heroes— Coop and Willie Boy—who symbolically are brothers. Willie Boy is Coop's doppelgänger, the dark twin to the luminous, but reluctant, enforcer of the law. Coop is careful, violent, as skilled in Indian ways as Willie Boy, but hesitant to assume his role. When he leaves for Riverside, he tells Ray that the posse "couldn't catch a dog in the street," that Willie Boy will not be found unless he wants to be, and that the matter is Indian business. For all these reasons Coop says, "The hell with him." Coop is avoiding his responsibilities.

Willie Boy is cunning, violent, and impetuous; he is a rebel in the screen tradition of James Dean in *Rebel without a Cause* and Marlon Brando in *The Wild One*. Willie Boy is confident and certain of who he is; his dialogue is uncompromising in his affirmation of his Indianness. There is no suggestion that he is an assimilationist, an Indian seeking to become part of the white world. Willie Boy does not need to undergo the mangling (*sparagmos*) or the recognition (*anagnorisis*) that Coop must.

Polonsky's portrayal of women is in accordance with long-standing Western film stereotypes. According to Tuska, "Women have changed externally in Western films during the last eight decades, with the trend always in the direction of revealing more and more of their bodies until total nudity was achieved; male attitudes concerning them, however, have changed very little."[9]

As Polonsky wrote them, Liz and Lola are the objects of male lust complicated by their additional roles as temptresses who try to deflect each hero from fulfilling his destiny. Liz both prevents Coop from doing his job and then shames him into action by claiming he is not the man his father was—he cannot even kill an Indian.

When Willie Boy runs off with Lola, Liz is angered because he has engaged in "marriage by capture." She claims, "It's the Paiute way and always was," but she rejects that Indian practice and wants Lola returned. Lola, says Liz, "didn't want to go with him, she doesn't want to be a desert squaw." Polonsky gives Lola the assimilationist lines and white dreams, having her yearn to be a schoolteacher like Liz and for Willie Boy to be a rancher. Lola wants Willie Boy to share her white dream; Willie Boy will have no part of it.

Willie Boy is also mythically dead from the film's beginning, which a series of verbal cues prepares us for. In the earliest dialogue we learn that Willie Boy worked on a ranch in Victorville for a white woman; he left when her husband returned. Race-mixing in Westerns is invariably punished by death, so this alerts us early on to Willie Boy's fate.[10] It is repeated when Old Mike says, "I can't hear you Willie Boy," reprised by the bunkmate asking Willie Boy what he is doing "ghosting around here" and made plain again when Willie Boy finds his father's "ghost shirt." Visually, we first see the ghostlike atmosphere in the moonlit orchard, and later we see it again when Willie Boy and Lola pass the posse in a mysterious fog.

Since Coop and Willie Boy are "brothers" and in conflict, the clash can only be resolved by death. Coop must recognize Willie Boy as his brother and touch him, his final *anagnorisis*. In the closing episode at Ruby Mountain, Coop sprawls in the mud to drink at a stream. He sees Willie Boy's handprint in the ooze and puts his own hand within it; the match is identical. Willie Boy lets Coop take him and makes of Coop his executioner. Willie Boy dies Indian, and Coop lives, having killed the myth, standing alone in the twilight of a frontier that has gone.

But Polonsky has no sympathy for those who view the past nostalgically, seeking to recall better days, and he drives his point home at the very end. The sheriff to whom Coop reports demands angrily to know who let the body be burned. "People'll want to see something," he growls, to which Coop's response is the last line spoken: "Tell them we're fresh out of souvenirs." Polonsky's deliberate word choice reflected his thinking. "Never mind all those souvenirs that they [nostalgia buffs, historians?] keep pushing down on us, all the sacrifices *they* made in the past," Polonsky told an interviewer. "I don't care about them. The past is not now. It's just a souvenir and we should not be bound by souvenirs."[11]

HISTORICAL ANALYSIS

From the historian's perspective, Polonsky's script and film have produced frustration and inaccuracy. Frustration arises from recognizing the profound difficulty in conveying historical issues when limited to expression through character development. A scene we admired on first read did not make the Final Screenplay, and we think we know why. The scene, set in Redlands, involves a farmer and his teenage son, sitting in a tree waiting for President Taft's motorcade. The boy is to throw lighted firecrackers at the car's wheels while the father chants protest slogans. There are even protesters in the crowd carrying placards. The protests, as written, are historically accurate. Why the frustration? Because what will such slogans as "Free Trade," "Down with Payne-Aldrich Act," and "Farmers-Ranchers against Taft" mean to a contemporary audience? To explain the background 65 to the scene or its significance within the film narrative would slow the story down and break up the flow. The audience cannot make an instant association with the Payne-Aldrich Act the way it can with the issues of presidential assassination or of sex. The scene, and a couple of others like it, were deleted from the Final Screenplay in favor of another interlude between Coop and Liz designed to show the meanness of white or "civilized" relationships between men and women.

Inaccuracies abound—some minor, some major, some caused by carelessness, others by the nature of the medium and the genre. Polonsky genuinely wanted to include Indians in his film. He used the Morongo Reservation to shoot several scenes and employed resident Cahuilla Indians in bit parts and in a scene where an Indian language is spoken, even though the incident occurred off the reservation and Cahuilla at Morongo had only limited involvement in the original drama.

In the poolroom scene there should have been no beer because Banning was a "dry" area in "dry" Riverside County. The same criticism applies later when the scene shifts to the Mission Inn in Riverside, where Coop is going to drink with members of the press in the bar and Liz serves champagne to her eastern associates. In 1909 Riverside County these things would not have happened.[12]

Since alcohol is important to the story, to illustrate both its bad effect on Indians and its consumption by whites, Polonsky took additional liberties. He invents an incident involving "blind piggers" — even though the historical Indian agent, Clara True, had driven them off the reservation with a fury — to show the role of the evil white man exploiting the Indian through drink. When Willie Boy tells Lola he served time in jail in San Bernardino, he says it was for being drunk. But that point, while asserted by Lawton and repeated by Polonsky, remains unproven. Polonsky has Willie Boy give his prison number as 273, although the photograph in Lawton's own collection shows Willie Boy's number was 674 (see fig. 5).[13]

Polonsky transformed the staid and very proper Clara True into the tall, lovely, and liberated Liz, a desert femme fatale, having a torrid affair with Redford's Coop. Someone who knew Clara True fairly well described her as "a short, dynamic, little old maid."[14] Clara True described herself this way: "I am not a suffragette, nor any sort of woman's rights advocate. I would not exchange the privileges I have for all the rights some women clamor for. I would not vote if I could."[15] A historically accurate Clara True would not do for story purposes. One of Lawton's correspondents discerned that fact early on, writing, "If Hollywood could jack up the love interest someplace by straining the truth, they could make a whale of a sensational picture out of the book, and no foolin! Of course, it would make a movie, for my money,

Fig. 5. Photograph of Willie Boy in county jail suit, ca. 1906 (Courtesy of Special Collections, Rivera Library, University of California, Riverside)

without embellishment, but you know Hollywood and SEX."[16]

This seemingly minor change by Polonsky, creating a different character altogether for the Indian agent from the actual historical person, takes on greater significance because he uses Liz and Coop, his one-man embodiment of the several posses, to comment on American relations between the oppositely attracted sexes. Liz and Coop are fictitious; Lola and Willie Boy were not. But in Polonsky's conception of them they are the embodiment of true heterosexual love. They harken to a past that has been lost.

To underscore that point in his final (draft) screenplay, Polonsky wanted the scene of confrontation with Lola's father to begin with a gnarled hand entering the scene, grabbing Lola by her hair, flinging her back. The clash would end with Old Mike sprawled on the ground as "the wild doves flutter fearfully in the almond trees, and Willie and Lola, naked and ghostlike, turn to each other like Adam and Eve on that fateful night in Eden." Even though the doves did not make the final print, the scene is crucially important to his story.

The imagery obviously suggests a myth beyond that of the American frontier. The Indian as "noble savage" teaches "civilized" whites the meaning of love. But the Indian fails; he is no longer prelapsarian because he, and she, commit Original Sin and are driven from the Orchard/Garden. Coop and the possemen are not just the agents of the city moving westward in America; more, they are God's own angels pursuing Willie Boy and Lola somewhere east of Eden. Since Willie Boy and Lola are to die, their lesson must die too. It is too late — we cannot learn, we cannot return to the Garden. Polonsky expands his biblical imagery at the end of the film when Coop, having brought Willie Boy's body back to burn, washes his bloody hands with the dirt of the West. Coop replays Pontius Pilate washing his hands of the death of Jesus of Nazareth, which means that Willie Boy has become a Christ figure, the ultimate innocent, destroyed by a corrupt world. What was good has been killed and is gone; only the fire remains.

The pessimistic message of the film bothered some American viewers and critics at the time. When President Taft visits Riverside, Sheriff Wilson announces that there will be no repeat of the McKinley assassination. Wilson thinks that easterners have lost touch with their origins; they do not know guns and how to use them the way westerners do. For an American audience in 1969, the irony of Polonsky's dialogue may have seemed mockery, given that President John F. Kennedy had been assassinated by rifle in the West in 1963 and his younger brother, Robert, murdered by gunfire in Los Angeles in 1968.

Polonsky's intended message, that "civilization is the process of despoiling, of *spoilation* of people, which in the past we considered a victory, but we now suspect is a moral defeat for all,"[17] raised the ire of *New Yorker* film critic Pauline Kael. Blaming American society for what it did to Indians, like Polonsky and others making pictures in the *Cinéma Rouge*, left viewers with only one way out of their collective guilt — Kael's "genosuicide." Well, she, for one, had

69

had enough! Kael thought that *Tell Them Willie Boy Is Here* might do well abroad and with "masochistic white Americans—the kind who want to believe that the corollary of 'Black is Beautiful' is 'White is Ugly.' "[18]

70 Indians criticized the film because of the failure to cast Indians in the leading Indian parts. Katherine Ross's comment that she did not want to play Lola like a typical "Hollywood Indian," no matter how well intended, was turned against her by critics, since she was just that: Hollywood's idea of what Lola *should* look like.[19] Robert Redford's fans had two other opportunities to see him on film in 1969, in *Butch Cassidy and the Sundance Kid* and *Downhill Racer*; in both movies he played confident, strong men in contrast to his characterization of the reluctant hero, Coop. In the more than twenty years that have elapsed since the film was released commercially, it has been played tens of thousands of times, in screenings of Westerns and Redford festivals, on college campuses, on television in the United States and abroad, and through videocassette rental and purchase. Even though Polonsky reversed Lawton's celebration of the West, making of the incident not a tribute to the posse but a dirge on the fate of civilization, the film version is undoubtedly better known than the book.

While the film disappoints as history, Tuska offers a reason why:

> A historical reconstruction, because it is fiction and not history, can embellish details based on the evidence *but it ought not at any point contradict the factual evidence.* Notwithstanding assertions to the

contrary by filmmakers and others, none of the films about . . . historical personalities dealt with in this section of the book has respected this rule; and, until this rule is respected in the scripting of Western films about historical personalities or events, it is folly to talk about using or interpreting history. What is being used, even exploited, is the ignorance of history on the part of the audience in order not to interpret, but to distort.[20]

Ironically, though, Polonsky's use of the Ghost Dance shirt, together with the existential ambiguity of Willie Boy's guilt for the deaths of Old Mike and Lola, suggests another approach to the story, an approach from Willie Boy's perspective. Polonsky even indicated, through his various screenplays, that he had begun to see beyond the falsehood of the restrictive word "Indian," to recognize that the term, like "white," covers a bafflingly diverse range of human beings.[21] Before we can pursue that line of inquiry, however, we must first determine if there is another possible perspective on Willie Boy from the white view, one that is at least less encumbered by myth than the novel or the film.

5

A Different White Man's Willie Boy

While Lawton romanticized the manhunt, placing it within the mythology of the frontier, Polonsky sought to debunk the romantic elements and to demythologize the past in his somber film. Both versions, however, were shaped by the myth of the frontier, either in celebration or in condemnation of it. But in each case significant parts of the story, recoverable from the white record, were either glossed over or not told. Those omissions, which we will evaluate as historians, give a richer and different version of events and prepare the way for seeking an Indian view. Let us begin with the white-recorded perception of Willie Boy.

Whites who knew Willie Boy agreed that he was a good worker. A longtime resident of Redlands, who knew Willie Boy only by his reputation, reported him to have been hard-working and sober.[1] Clara True, the Indian agent at the Morongo Reservation in Banning, made the same observation in writing her report on the incident. She speculated further that he may have been the "grandson of a chief."[2] Regardless of accuracy, her statement suggested that Willie Boy was a high-status Indian.

Lawton interviewed some longtime residents in the course of his research, and they had similar observations. Jim McInnis remembered that his father engaged Willie Boy to cut juniper wood for the Hesperia Land and Water Company at different times over a period of two or three years. McInnis described Willie Boy as "a lone wolf. He would just drop in out of space and always find a cutting job open. He would stay two or three months, collect his pay and leave. He was no talker either."[3]

James Goulding first met Willie Boy when the Indian was helping Sam Rogers, who lived above Victorville, put up alfalfa. Goulding was impressed with Willie Boy's work. Later, Willie Boy and a group of six or eight Indians, consisting of several women, children, and two or three males, passed through Lucerne Valley on their way to gather pine nuts (*piñones*). Goulding needed help then in harvesting his own alfalfa crop and succeeded in prevailing upon Willie Boy to turn away from the group and assist.

When Goulding's small daughter decided to follow Willie Boy's lead and drink water from an irrigation ditch, the father scolded the girl. Although Goulding "felt sorry to hear" about Willie Boy's trouble with the law and thought that "as an Indian he was making good," Goulding was no Indian sympathizer. To Goulding, Willie Boy "was reasonably quiet for that breed of dog. I hadn't much use for Indians, since some of my best friends had been shot by them and that sort of thing sticks in your craw."[4]

Even one of the white possemen, Joe Toutain, had held a good opinion of Willie Boy. Nearly fifty years after the manhunt, and ten years following Ben de Crevecoeur's death, Toutain spoke publicly about his opinion of Willie Boy's character. For a few years before the incident, Toutain had hired Willie Boy as a cowboy. "We always had been good friends," Toutain told John Q. Copeland in 1957. "We ate from the same stew kettle on cattle roundups. We shared bedroll space under the chuck wagon during storms."[5]

Privately, Toutain admitted that he respected Willie Boy. Toutain had remained silent over the years, gone along with the negative images of the "bad Indian" articulated by Reche and especially by de Crevecoeur, because Toutain lived in Banning and the townspeople would not tolerate speaking well of Willie Boy.[6] For Toutain, the episode occurred because on that occasion, Willie Boy was "a man who just couldn't hold his liquor."[7] This charge demands further investigation.

At the time of the episode, then, Willie Boy generally was seen by whites as hard-working, not a drinker, somewhat aloof from other Indians, and of probable high-status. The drinking episode described later by de Crevecoeur surprised locals because they had not previously associated Willie Boy with alcohol. As noted in chapter 2, de Crevecoeur made this charge fifteen days after the incident began and four days following the ambush at Ruby Mountain.

The long delay in making the disclosure invites suspicion. If Willie Boy had been drunk, or if he had been drinking prior to the confrontation, why did Maria, the girl's mother and the wife of the man who Willie Boy killed, not mention it at the time? The alcohol abuse charge originated in the confession of an unidentified white youth. De Crevecoeur's story was clever; the white boy had hidden liquor in the bunkhouse he shared with Willie Boy, and de Crevecoeur surmised that the Indian had found and drank it prior to his confrontation with the old man. The story is clever because no one confessed to selling or giving the Indian liquor and therefore the confessant would not have been subject to prosecution. De Crevecoeur then appeared generous in not revealing the youth's identity. And no one actually saw Willie Boy consume the alcohol. The liquor was simply made conveniently available, and the stereotypical Indian weakness for alcohol took over white imagination.

What could de Crevecoeur possibly gain from this story? Drunkenness became both an explanation of Willie Boy's behavior and the reason why the posse needed to return to the manhunt to confirm or deny his suicide. Locals knew of the reputation for drunkenness among the Morongo Indians prior to Clara True's arrival, a reputation to which de Crevecoeur's story appealed, although Willie Boy was not a local Indian.

Unpunished Indian drunkenness, nevertheless, could not be tolerated by representatives of the Bureau of

Indian Affairs, and Ben de Crevecoeur was a probationary U.S. special officer in 1909. The next year he would be reviewed to determine if he should have a regular appointment. Having the Willie Boy case resolved and his role in it acknowledged would have helped advance de Crevecoeur to a regular post.

Following the ambush, however, the possemen did not want to return to Ruby Mountain. Additional prodding was needed to get another posse to ride, and de Crevecoeur's tale contributed to that remount. He also succeeded in agitating Clara True, who, in turn, did her utmost to get men back in the saddle to close the case. It would have been unwise for de Crevecoeur to return to Ruby Mountain alone for two reasons: if Willie Boy was not dead, another posse would be needed anyway to continue the pursuit; if he was dead, de Crevecoeur's trip would have been unglamorous.

With the assignment of Randolph Madison to the last posse, de Crevecoeur had a piece of unexpected good fortune to assure press coverage of his activities. By ingratiating himself with Madison, de Crevecoeur had the opportunity for "hogging headlines," which Reche deplored. But the reporting proved good for the probationary officer. In 1910 de Crevecoeur's appointment as federal special officer was made permanent.[8]

With the appearance of de Crevecoeur's story, Willie Boy's earlier reputation was set aside in retellings of the episode. But that earlier reputation had been won by hard work and sobriety, a reputation conferred upon Willie Boy by disinterested whites, by those who had nothing to gain in speaking well of an Indian, by those who would have spoken well of Willie Boy only if his behavior had been, in some way to them, remarkable.

Given de Crevecoeur's self-interest in the liquor story and the fact that it began and ended with him—there was no one else identifiable who could corroborate it—we could drop it from any retelling as unproven but for Lawton's later claim to have found a corroborating witness. This is strange. De Crevecoeur's alleged informant acted alone, but fifty years later, another man confessed to being an accomplice.

Lawton added another youth to de Crevecoeur's account, giving him the fictitious name of Bill Holden. In so doing and in claiming that de Crevecoeur knew him, Lawton changed de Crevecoeur's story.[9] By then, de Crevecoeur was dead and in no position to argue. Yet, since he insisted on a lone white youth as perpetrator and because he knew the identity of "Bill Holden," then "Holden" was not his man.

Who was "Holden," and why should his story be any more credible than de Crevecoeur's? In the notes Lawton prepared for his manuscript, which became *Willie Boy: A Desert Manhunt,* Lawton initially used the single name Robles, which he also described as fictitious, for the figure who became "Bill Holden." Someone reading the manuscript for Lawton, upon encountering the name "Robles," underlined it twice and wrote in the margin, "Some kind of slip Harry?"[10] The reader thought that Lawton had inadvertently revealed the name of his informant; but Lawton had not.[11]

In 1958 Otto Sweeters told Lawton, "I'm the guy responsible for getting W[illie] B[oy] drunk." With those words Sweeters began a story remarkably close to the one de Crevecoeur frequently told. Now, however, instead of one youth there were two. Sweeters claimed to have accompanied a Cliff Cheney to San Bernardino for an outing. It might have been a circus, but he did not remember. They bought a quart bottle of whiskey at a saloon and took the last train back to Banning; while riding, they consumed a quarter of the bottle. Once back in town, Sweeters claimed to have told Cheney to take the remainder of the bottle with him and to hide it up in the Gilman Ranch bunkhouse where Cheney was staying. Since Willie Boy slept in the other room, Sweeters surmised that he had seen Cheney return and hide the bottle. When the boys later learned of the killing of William Mike and the kidnap of his daughter, they concluded that Willie Boy had stolen the bottle and the rifle from the bunkhouse. Terrified that they might be arrested for letting the whiskey fall into Willie Boy's hands, they promised never to mention it again. Sweeters told Lawton that he had told only his wife.[12]

Sweeters "confessed" to Lawton a decade after de Crevecoeur's death, which meant that his account could not be checked against the originator of the tale. Lawton intended to follow up and locate the Cliff Cheney whom Sweeters mentioned, but apparently Lawton never did. While Sweeters's confession contradicted some details of de Crevecoeur's story, it confirmed the end result and added a witness.

Although dead and unable to respond, why might de Crevecoeur have objected to this new information? Several reasons come to mind. De Crevecoeur's account, as we noted, was self-contained and could not be contradicted. It did not even need the white youth, who may have been a de Crevecoeur invention. Sweeters's version raised doubts. Now instead of one boy hiding liquor in the bunkhouse, two were involved. Neither version of the story delivers what each claims. At the time of the manhunt the *San Bernardino Daily Sun* proclaimed, "Temperance Lesson in Blood, Drink Fest Is Cause of All the Trouble Brought on by Fugitive Indian." Half a century later Sweeters told Lawton that he was "the guy responsible for getting W[illie] B[oy] drunk." In each case the story adds up to placing whiskey in the proximity of Willie Boy; rather than witnesses, only white imagination sees him drinking it.

White imagination about Indians and alcohol, a substance introduced by fur traders who taught Indians how to abuse it, had ready stereotypes to invoke. As Native American Michael Dorris has written: "Drinking in sprees, drinking everything in sight when it was available (with intermittent periods of abstinence), drinking until drunkenness turned into unconsciousness—all part and parcel of the European introduced trading ritual—became the hallmark of popular American folk belief about the way Indians 'naturally' responded to alcohol."[13] Popular stereotype substituted for evidence when an allegation was made concerning Willie Boy and whiskey.

Sweeters's "confession" is as believable as de Crevecoeur's story; each seeks to establish guilt with nothing more convincing than possible association. Why Sweeters would have confessed to something he did not do is a subject for the sociologists and psychologists who study victimology.[14]

In the context of the Willie Boy story, however, the unproven liquor episode is important in understanding the metaphysics of Indian-hating. To vilify a previously well-regarded Indian, it was necessary for whites to determine that Willie Boy's character was fundamentally evil. A rampage begun by a drunken Indian intensified Indian villainy and enhanced posse virtue. Even though the alleged liquor episode surfaced late in the manhunt, two-thirds of the subsequent retellings begin the incident with alcohol (see Appendix).

Just as liquor contributes to the Indian-hating elements of the story, so also does the appearance of the president. William Howard Taft's visit to San Bernardino, Redlands, and Riverside on October 12, 1909, coincided with the Willie Boy manhunt. Reporters accompanying the president had become bored by the lack of news and, when writers for two New York newspapers—the *Sun* and the *World*—learned of the chase, they wrote about it for their eastern readers.[15] The combined daily circulation of those papers was more than 455,000 copies, compared with local newspaper circulation of about 10,000 and 145,000 in Los Angeles.[16]

While Taft's visit brought Willie Boy to the attention of the East, local California papers were incensed at the coverage eastern papers gave them. The *Riverside Morning Mission* had imagined the kind of glowing account that easterners might have read: "Through dustless streets cool with the grateful shade of the tropical pepper tree, air laden with the fragrance of orange and lemon blossoms, President Taft today rode among the world famed orange groves of Riverside. It was the most delightful day the President had spent. It was the most beautiful city Mr. Taft had seen." As the *Mission* noted, however, "It didn't work out quite that way."[17]

The reporter for the *Sun* dubbed Riverside "Willie Boy Country" and devoted two-thirds of his story to the Indian's misdeeds. The *World* also spent too much time on Willie Boy to suit the *Mission* and, even more insulting to local boosters, described Taft's automobile visit as dust plagued, preventing the president from seeing the local beauty and causing him to arrive at a Glenwood banquet with "eyes red." "Willie Boy," the *Mission* bitterly concluded," makes better 'copy' in New York than beautiful Riverside or a Glenwood banquet."[18]

Local newspapers wanted the eastern press to ignore the manhunt—which local papers had exploited to increase circulation—and to write instead of local beauty. But local newspapers could not have it both ways. They could not simultaneously appeal to Indian-hating through sensationalized reporting and then cry foul when outsiders chose to cover a story that local newspapers had themselves generated.

There was no danger to the president, yet the eastern newsmen sensed an affinity in the local story with the nation's leader. Taft and Willie Boy shared an affinity intrinsic to the myth of the frontier, to the story of "civilization" from the city taming "savage" nature. Willie Boy as drunken murderer embodied the unruliness of the wild that the city sought to subdue; Taft as president embodied the city, symbolizing the "civilization" that Willie Boy challenged. The New York papers focused eastern attention on a part of the West where American "civilization," as the writers implied, had not yet prevailed.

Local papers at the time used Taft's visit to spur reluctant men to reform a posse, and Taft's visit has been related, beginning with Lawton's book, in seven of the subsequent retellings.[19] Not surprisingly, given Taft's symbolism, law enforcement accounts compose half of the versions that incorporate the presidential trip.

Polonsky made the unseen president a significant part of his film, a vehicle for airing the director's views on violence and presidential assassination as well as a reason why Redford's character, Sheriff Coop, is diverted from his duties. Thus happenstance—an irrelevant coincidence between a presidential visit and an episode in local law enforcement—has proven important to the Willie Boy tale because of its value for the frontier myth.

Other misperceptions have frustrated an attempt to re-create the Willie Boy incident from a historical perspective. One involved Carlota's desire to go to school, which Willie Boy's kidnap allegedly prevented her from doing. In this version it is Willie Boy's cruelty that sought to prevent her uplift through white knowledge.[20] Lawton in his book and Polonsky in his film both have her express a wish to go to school. Clara True, the film's Liz Arnold, ostensibly originated these reports.

True, however, never encouraged the young woman to pursue the goal and remarked, "I did not comment on the school idea but watched the development of it with interest. . . . I did not know whether going to school would make a girl of her age happier."[21] Clara True, in not deciding, decided; education would be of dubious value to Carlota. So Clara True, not Willie Boy, prevented Carlota from pursuing a white education. By blaming Willie Boy, however, Indian-hating is reinforced; yet another piece of "evidence" is marshaled to prove his "bad" character.

Clara True, concerned that if Willie Boy were not captured quickly, other Indians would join him, stirred up local fear of an Indian revolt. The uprising and massacre at Wounded Knee in 1890 occurred twenty years before the Willie Boy incident; George Armstrong Custer had been defeated at the Little Big Horn a mere fourteen years earlier, in 1876. For many people in Southern California those incidents had immediacy, and the threat of another large-scale Indian-white confrontation frightened people.

More than eighty years after the manhunt, Donald S. C. Anderson, who was nine years old at the time and living with his family in Redlands, vividly remembered daily discussions over the dinner table of the pursuit. He remembered helping his father and other adult neighbors clean their firearms in anticipation of an Indian attack. He and his classmates walking to school worried that Willie Boy might get them.[22]

Thus when local and regional newspapers reported that Indian agents in Southern California and Arizona were closely watching their charges and keeping their superiors in Washington alert to prevent any outbreak by Paiutes and Chemehuevis in support of the outlaw, those newspapers appealed to white fear.[23] In part, fear spurred the posse to return to Ruby Mountain after the shoot-out.

Clara True provided the press with these reports because no other source for them in local or national archives could be found. She was the only agent to express this fear.[24] Press reports that the army was on alert to counter this danger were simple prevarications. Had the army been involved in any way, mention of it would have been made in the reports of the respective commands to the War Department. The department's annual report contains no mention of Willie Boy or of any suspected or real Indian trouble in the affected areas.[25]

One further extraneous misperception involves Lawton's claim that this was "the last western manhunt,"[26] in which "the Wild West was revived for one last florid curtain call by the Willie Boy affair."[27] Burr Belden, a fellow journalist at the *San Bernardino Sun* and author of over one thousand articles on local history, tried to qualify Lawton's exaggeration by pointing out that Lawton's description was "undoubtedly correct as far as the Mojave Desert is concerned."[28] While there is little doubt that this was the biggest manhunt in San Bernardino and Riverside counties to that date, a larger claim seems possible only from the writings and photographs of Madison that informed Lawton's book.

Madison's stories, however, written after the entire drama had transpired, do not appear to have had much impact. The *St. Louis Post Dispatch* carried them on October 9 and 16, but the *Chicago Tribune* did not. And the *New York Times* devoted only a tiny story to the manhunt on October 10 and reported Willie Boy's suicide a week later in a quarter-column next to a report headlined "Golf Ball Hurts Actress." As important as this episode may have seemed to locals at the time, it appears that Lawton's novel and Polonsky's film deserve the credit for making it "the last great western manhunt."

Such language betrays a fallacy that Patricia Nelson Limerick's *Legacy of Conquest* challenges us all to reconsider. Whether it is the image of the "vanishing American" or of "the last great western manhunt," the idea we are being asked to accept is that a sharp discontinuity exists between the contemporary West and the historic West. But Lawton's book and Polonsky's film both belie that argument, since each advances a view of the West as fable, the result of which has inflated a local tale into regional lore that has become part of the mythic West. Both novel and film share an unconscious contribution to the perpetuation of Indian-hating, and in that shared contribution, each confirms Limerick's idea of continuity between past and present in the West.

Indian-hating, which has allowed the embellishments and misperceptions of the Willie Boy incident to persist, has helped to thwart a re-creation of this episode from an Indian perspective. Encrustations on the story alternately aggravate white fears of sudden, unprovoked Indian violence and allay white consciences that what befell Willie Boy was morally right. In the prevailing version of the story, Willie Boy got what he deserved; questioning the accuracy of the story could be dismissed as deranged or sentimental Indian sympathizing.

The story as it stands reduces Indians to stereotypes and prevents their being seen as actors in their own past. We thus must turn to ethnohistory to continue the story. We enter the field knowing our limitations and liabilities.

6

Trying to Enter a Numinous Land

Early in the course of our research, a mutual friend referred us to Joe Benitez, a Chemehuevi living on the Cabazon Reservation who was a grandson of William Mike. Our friend had called him a chief.[1] We thought that in talking to Joe, we would be the first whites to converse with a member of the family Willie Boy had disrupted in 1909.

We were not. Long after our dialogue with Joe had begun, we discovered that Harry Lawton had donated the papers he had gathered from his Willie Boy project to the University of California at Riverside. In those papers we learned that Lawton had talked with Dorothy "Dot" Rogers, a younger sister of Carlota and Joe Benitez's aunt. Lawton, for reasons known only to himself, did not pursue that line of inquiry.[2] He did, however, insert some of the information he had learned from Dot Rogers in *Willie Boy: A Desert Manhunt,* and we will turn to that material at the end of this chapter.

Joe Benitez advised us to contact his cousin Adrian Fisher, living on the Colorado River Indian Tribes (CRIT) reservation at Parker, Arizona. Both Joe and Adrian had been chairman of their respective tribal councils; both men were chiefs. Their authority, between Indio, California, and Parker, Arizona, bracketed the story's geography. When we met Adrian, he in turn introduced us to Chemehuevis living near the river who belonged either to Willie Boy's family or to the Mikes. Together, Joe and Adrian gave us access to members of both families who had either direct knowledge of or lore about the story. The chiefs granted us that access to bring the Chemehuevi version forward.

In integrating our own fieldwork with printed ethnographic materials, we wish to present the results of our efforts in a way that makes the process of doing ethnohistory more accessible to the reader. We begin by establishing some ethnographic background from published and unpublished sources. Then we have chosen to put the narrative of our most important field trip and conversations with Chemehuevis in italic form; we alternate in plain text with amplifications on that material from the background sources.

Because Willie Boy is at the center of the tale, we think it important to begin by considering his background. The supervisor of Indian Schools for the region in 1909 described Willie Boy as a mixed-blood Paiute and Chemehuevi who lived at Twentynine Palms, where William Mike and his family also resided.[3] Supervisor Harwood Hall followed the convention of identifying the tribe of the father, followed by that of the mother, in his description of Willie Boy.

Clara True, Indian agent at Morongo, wrote, "Willie Boy grew up a desert man, sinewy and healthy. He never had any training except that of the desert and the little he picked up at infrequent times when he came in toward the towns and worked a short time for wages. He spoke English rather well but never associated with the Spanish population enough to learn Spanish. . . . he was well dressed, did not drink in any noticeable quantity and did not gamble."[4]

What would this "training" of the desert have been like? What would it have meant for Willie Boy? Answers to those questions lie in the ethnography of the people with whom he was reared: the Chemehuevi. Information important in establishing Willie Boy's background came from work done by people associated with the celebrated and eccentric anthropologist John Peabody Harrington. In the summer of 1919, ten years after the Willie Boy manhunt, Harrington's wife, Carobeth, met George Laird, a mixed-blood white-Cherokee and Chemehuevi, from whom she chose to learn and study the Chemehuevi language.

Shortly thereafter she divorced Harrington, married Laird, and went to live among the Chemehuevi. To affirm their uniqueness in a region of overlapping Indian groups, the Chemehuevi called themselves The People, a widespread practice among native peoples. Although George Laird died in 1940, Carobeth continued to live with the Chemehuevi, and she took notes on their culture and language all her life.[5]

Carobeth's daughter by Harrington, Awonawilona, wrote the first ethnographic study based upon extensive fieldwork among the Chemehuevi, which she completed in 1934. She sent it to her father to aid him in his work. The name Chemehuevi, she noted, came from a Mojave word said to mean "mixed with all" and was applied to the Chemehuevi and to Southern Paiutes, whose territory overlapped.

The Chemehuevi, as a distinct group, were highly intermingled; according to Awonawilona, they possessed a love of change and of learning to "speak strange tongues, sing strange songs, and marry strange wives." While they were nomadic and given to change, they maintained their sense of identity and culture because of an intense pride that she described as "arrogance and conceit."

"Their pleasure in the acquisition of foreign languages was balanced by their pride in their own rich, intricate tongue," she wrote. As a group, they prized agility and swiftness over physical strength, and a common practice of Southern Fox, a mythic hero, was to outrun and dodge his own arrows. The Chemehuevi were "inclined to friendship by their unquenchable curiosity about the customs and affairs of others as well as by a natural kindliness. . . . no other tribes, however, felt more strongly in the matter of revenge."[6]

Awonawilona Harrington's observations spoke to the problematic term "Paiute," which, in the first three decades of this century, was applied indiscriminately to groups with significant tribal differences. Distinguished anthropologist Alfred Kroeber early noted the importance of differentiating the Chemehuevi from the Paiute, either Northern or Southern, to distinguish them from other tribes in California, Nevada, Arizona, or Utah.[7] Although "bride capture" was not unknown among the Ute and Shoshone, which were encompassed by the term "Paiute," it was rare; weapons were not used, nor was violence employed to take the woman. And the practice did not exist among these people in California.[8] This "Indian custom" came solely from reporter Randolph Madison in 1909, derived no doubt from Ben de Crevecoeur, an example perhaps of the eastern-born and aristocratic Madison's noblesse oblige, undercut by Indian-hating.

Lawton, seeking to confirm Madison's "Paiute" custom story, found a single example of Ute bride capture involving murder with a rifle and used it as an epigraph to begin his version of the story, thus implying that it was a widespread cultural practice. Polonsky in turn incorporated the idea into *Tell Them Willie Boy Is Here*. Thus bride capture, which became important in retelling the story, was not even created until after the story was over. If there had been some such custom among the Chemehuevi at Twentynine Palms, Clara True would have mentioned it in her report. Hence Tom Hughes's observation that storytellers have attached crimes and behavior to Willie Boy over the years "out of pure generosity" seems apt.

Carobeth Laird's years of insight, developed from observation and discussion with George Laird and many other Chemehuevis, enabled her to compose a book that treated the language, customs, culture, and religion of these people in far greater detail than had her daughter, Awonawilona. In the matter of court-ship, Chemehuevi culture did not practice bride ab-duction. There were two ways for contracting mar-riage with a young girl or woman who still lived with her parents. The more formal method involved the suitor approaching the girl's father; if the father thought he was of good character, talks continued. The alter-native method was for a male cousin to take the suitor with him on a visit to the girl's family. That night the cousin would lie down by the girl next to the fire to discuss the situation. If she agreed, the cousin yielded his place to the suitor, and in the morning, her parents awoke to find the union already consummated.[9]

> *On February 15, 1991, we drove out Interstate High-way 10 past Banning and through the San Gorgonio Pass that divides the Peninsular from the Transverse mountain ranges, the land surfaces which shape the climate of Southern California.[10] At State Highway 62 we turned north, heading out toward the desert and Twentynine Palms. As we drove across the desert, we tried to imagine how the Chemehuevis eighty years ago saw the land. Beyond Twentynine Palms we passed imperceptibly from the High to the Low Desert as the terrain of the Mojave descends toward the river. The average annual rainfall in each part of the desert is less than ten inches, even less than five inches in the Low Desert, but the significant change is the tem-perature.[11]*

Desert dwellers must adapt to land having little water, to rugged and varied terrain, and to tempera-ture extremes of intense heat at midday and near-freezing cold at midnight. Knowledge of usable water sources was critical to life. Without the technological advantages of the late twentieth century, survival depended upon intimate knowledge of the land, a thorough familiarity with desert plant and animal life. The Chemehuevi shared part of the riverine environment with the more numerous and hostile Mojave. The Mojave belonged to the Yuman-speaking Indian group, known for their ferocity in battle. These people had challenged Spanish penetration of the river in the eighteenth century and had temporarily closed the overland route from New Spain (Mexico) into Alta California by their warfare. Thus the Chemehuevi had to cope with hostile neighbors as well as a sere environment.

The key to individual Chemehuevi survival lay in the personal knowledge of a hereditary song that defined kinship groups and territorial hunting rights. A song generally was passed from father to son, but if a woman married a non-Chemehuevi (i.e., a man without a song), then her son inherited her father's song. A man could know more than one song, but his hereditary song, the song he owned, defined and limited his hunting preserve.

From a Euro-American perspective, these songs constituted a map, for they enabled the singer to orient himself to a terrain that might frequently seem to Euro-Americans to be featureless. By repetition and inflection, by use of special names for certain geographic features, a Chemehuevi singer could find water, shelter, and edible plants to aid him in his search for game.

The two most important of these hereditary songs remaining in the time of George Laird (1871–1940) were those of the mountain sheep, covering territory west of the Colorado River, and those of the deer, which ranged over land lying east of the river.[12] George Laird's descriptions of aspects of Chemehuevi culture, especially his ability to link customs to time, permit us to apply some of his insights historically.

George Laird told Carobeth of a particular cult that, by the turn of the century, he said was on the wane — the cult of the runners. It had probably derived from older times when a chief needed special messengers to bear his staff and communicate his messages to other chiefs very quickly across the desert. The runners were extraordinary in their physical ability to traverse large sections of desert with little or no water and at very high speed.

By about 1900 only one group of runners remained, agile young men who ran together for the joy of it and who called each other cousin. Among this group was one youth who knew "the secret way of traveling, which was the old way." He was quiet and gentle in demeanor, never boisterous, and when he ran with his friends, he ran as they did. When he ran alone, however, he ran the secret way, appearing at his destination almost simultaneously with his departure.

Someone outside Chemehuevi culture might skeptically think this a claim to teleportation. George Laird, however, insisted that it was a secret involving ancient methods of body and mind control, not magic. One day when this runner chose to travel alone, some of his companions decided to track him. "They followed his tracks up to and over the crest of the dune to the point where they had lost sight of him. The tracks continued on, but now they were different. They looked as if he had been 'just staggering along,' taking giant steps, his feet touching the ground at long, irregular intervals, leaving prints that became further and further apart and lighter and lighter on the sand." The young men changed direction and quit tracking.[13]

"Indian runners," as anthropologist Peter Nabokov phrased it, "relied on powers beyond their own abilities to help them run for war, hunting, and sport. To dodge, maintain long distances, spurt for shorter ones, to breathe correctly and transcend oneself called for a relationship with strengths and skills which were the property of animals, trails, stars and elements. Without their tutelage and beneficence one's potential could never be realized."[14]

These elements in the ethnohistory of the Chemehuevi seem germane to Willie Boy. His extraordinary endurance in outrunning a mounted posse—running at least two marathons over desert sand and rock without water and carrying a rifle—has already been noted. At points in his flight his strides lengthened to between five and seven feet,[15] a feat nothing short of miraculous by white standards but a phenomenon associated with the runners and reflecting a combination of knowledge and ability possessed by only a few. We provisionally conclude that Willie Boy must have been a runner in the old Chemehuevi tradition. Perhaps conversations with the Chemehuevi at Parker can confirm or deny this ability.

It would seem that George Laird, ten years older than Willie Boy, must have known the younger lad. Neither Carobeth nor Awoniwilona, however, asked

George Laird about Willie Boy. And, at the time each woman gathered information, George Laird frequently invoked the Chemehuevi taboo against speaking the name of the dead. This taboo was well on the wane when Carobeth published her book in 1976, but the earlier practice encouraged individuals to forget the names of even close relatives. George Laird had even forgotten his own mother's Chemehuevi name, for example, by the time he talked with Carobeth, because his mother had died when he was six.[16]

Patrick Lyttle looked at us silently, his arms crossed over his chest, as we sat talking to two Indian women on either side of him at the Blue Water Landing Cafe overlooking the river outside of Parker, Arizona. In the course of our waiting for Adrian, these two women from the CRIT Library and Museum (Amelia Flores, director, and Bonita Stevens, curator), had sought us out to talk. They were concerned with what we were doing. Had we obtained permission from the tribal council to talk with any of the Indians out here? They knew how popular Dances With Wolves *had been, especially among their own people. Were we making a movie? Who in Hollywood did we represent? Would we share sources and exchange information with the museum archives?*

We assured them that although we lived in Southern California, we had no Hollywood connections and did not know Kevin Costner. We explained our relationship to Adrian, the role of Joe Benitez in getting us to Parker, and the purpose of our inquiry: to try to determine a Chemehuevi perspective on the Willie Boy episode. We talked in general terms about George and Carobeth Laird but without revealing any of the specific detail presented above.

After sitting silently for nearly half an hour, Patrick unfolded his arms and declared: "I'm going to talk to them. When Adrian told me about them, to talk to them, I thought, 'Well, I'm going to see for myself; make up my own mind.' I have listened. They are doing right. They are asking about Indian stories of this Willie Boy thing. I say this. My mother told me that I am a descendant of runners. Willie Boy was a runner too." Our inference about Willie Boy had been confirmed.

Are there still runners, we asked? Patrick shook his head. Bonita added, "Today we drive."

Patrick then talked of differences between Chemehuevi and other river tribes. Noting that he is one of the very few who can still speak the old Chemehuevi language, he talked about particular Chemehuevi traits that irritate other Indians. He began with their humor. "We are always joking with people and language. We do slangy things, and sometimes other Indians think we are talking bad about them—but we aren't." Amelia, who is Mojave, agreed, saying that even after several years working with Bonita and Patrick, she is still not adjusted to their sense of humor.

According to Patrick (and Bonita agreed), the Chemehuevi have an ironic way of looking at sad events or death "that doesn't sit well with other Indians. It's not that we aren't serious. And we show no disrespect. But we can see humor even in sadness. And we are different. At powwows and get-togethers, Indians sometimes dance in each other's ceremonies. But not me. I stick to Chemehuevi. I am Chemehuevi and proud to be Chemehuevi."

We asked if he had heard of the Ghost Dance. He thought for a minute in silence. "I'm translating it," he said. "It's old Chemehuevi. I know some songs, I know I sang them when I was a little kid. Been a long time. From the older people you know. I'll try to remember. But they wouldn't mean nothing to you."

Some individual runners particularly were the most profoundly influenced by the revival of the Ghost Dance religion in 1890–91. The Ghost Dance, which began about 1870 and was revived twenty years later, started within a group of Paviotso, or Northern Paiute, in the Mason Valley of Nevada. In popular thought the Ghost Dance is associated with the uprising among the Sioux at the Pine Ridge and Rosebud reservations in South Dakota, which led to the tragic massacre at Wounded Knee in late December 1890. Because of the antiwhite message associated with the diffusion of the cult among the Plains Indians, the peaceful nature of the original message and its origin among nonwarlike peoples have frequently been overlooked. The Paiute formulation of the message, however, was far different from the Plains Indian interpretation.

Wovoka, whose father had been a disciple of the first Ghost Dance,[17] had a vision in which he died and went to heaven. There he saw "all the people who had died a long time ago. God told me to come back and tell my people that they must be good and love one another and not fight, or steal, or lie. He gave me this dance to give to my people."[18] Wovoka's message about whites was clear: Indians should learn or borrow from them those ways that were good and should shun those ways that were bad. Alcohol was a substance of the whites that Indians should not touch.[19]

The conventional method for disseminating the Prophet's message was for a tribal representative to visit and talk with him in Nevada, then return to the tribe and describe in detail not only what Wovoka said but how he looked and acted.[20] It is difficult to assess the extent of impact of the Ghost Dance upon the Chemehuevi because George Laird's is the only recorded reaction to it. He danced it "for fun," for the sociability of congregating in group assembly.

As Laird recalled, it all began with the passing of a pipe among river tribes from north to south, and when all the Chemehuevi had smoked it, they passed it on. About a year later, in 1891, the first Ghost Dance songs appeared. Decades afterward, an aspect of the teaching that Laird could remember was that the world was soon to be destroyed by fire and that only those who danced the Ghost Dance would survive.[21]

But George Laird also remembered that when the Ghost Dance revival came among the Chemehuevi living along the Colorado River, several chiefs came together to confer. Many Indians heard a voice, each speaking in his own tongue or sacred song, chiefs as well as braves, ordinary people, mixed-bloods, shamans, and especially the runners. While George Laird was unimpressed with the Ghost Dance, others felt deeply influenced by it. In one family, two young men failed to learn their traditional, hereditary Deer Song in favor of becoming Ghost Dance singers. From George Laird's recollection, the Ghost Dance had its greatest effect upon those who owned the Deer Song, among whom were most of the runners.[22]

An indication of the Ghost Dance's impact upon an individual can be seen in its effect upon John Smith, Laird's half-brother. Smith sought to become a Ghost Dance singer and participated seriously in the rituals. He grew progressively more satisfied with his new dreams until he began to dream of instructions for healing the sick, a signal that he could be summoned to become a shaman. Smith did not believe he wanted to accept the responsibility of a medicine man, so he told his dreams. In that act he broke the change process and became neither shaman nor Ghost Dancer. But he did retain his hereditary song.[23]

The Ghost Dance teaching prompted other Chemehuevis, including runners, to leave the river community to go alone or in small groups to live closer to whites for a while. Such a departure, which could be temporary, did not necessarily mean loss or renunciation of the hereditary song. But when Ghost Dance songs substituted for hereditary songs, the Ghost Dance contributed to Chemehuevi cultural change.[24] The Ghost Dance inspired hope. Wovoka's message was of "renewal, rebirth, and revitalization . . . that all Indians—living and dead—would be reunited in a world paradise, where Indians would be eternally free from poverty, disease, and death."[25]

"The posse never got him, you know. He got away to Nevada. He died in a sanitorium in Lofton in 1947, I believe. But ask Mary Lou, she knows." We were seated in a living room in the town of Parker, talking with Alberta Van Fleet. She is a health worker for the CRIT and Adrian has brought us to her house. Alberta is a descendant of Willie Boy's family.

She and Adrian bantered good-naturedly as we asked questions. "What if," we ask, "somehow Willie Boy really did die? What if he left Carlota alive and returned to find her dead. Could he then have committed suicide? If he did, would that have been considered an act of cowardice?" Alberta shook her head and said, "No, I don't think so." Adrian said, "Well, it could be interpreted that way." Alberta kidded, "If we bring that up again, Adrian, we might begin fighting."

On a sofa in Parker, Arizona, eighty years after the fact, descendants of Willie Boy's and the Mike families talked about the incident to interested whites. Alberta remembered that her mother would talk about it from time to time; Adrian recalled that Joe's family had more of that lore. Alberta told us that while her mother was very ill, about two years ago, a member of the Mike family came and stayed with her, looked after the elder while Alberta worked. The Mike family member nursed Alberta's mother through to the end.

At the time of our visit, Alberta was nursing a Mike family member who has been injured and disabled. We asked if the rift between the two families had now been mended. Alberta nodded, "That's right, it has finally healed now."

Willie Boy was ten when the revived Ghost Dance was transmitted among the Chemehuevi, an age when hearing a voice from on high could have been particularly moving. As a runner learning the secrets of an ancient cult that was then in decline, the message of renewal preached by Wovoka would have offered hope. The Ghost Dance religion offered the comfort that the living would be reunited with the dead in a new harmony.

When enumerated in the 1900 census, nineteen-year-old Willie Boy was living in Victor Township, now Victorville, with his sister, Georgia, and her family. He had taken the responsibility for two boys, identified simply as Indian Bill, eight, and Indian Albert, six, both of whom were orphans and from another tribe.[26]

In Chemehuevi myth there is a story called "How Cottontail Rabbit Conquered the Sun" in which the animal protagonist, in the course of his quest, encounters two orphaned human children. Cottontail Rabbit takes care of the orphans, and when he completes his task, humankind can live on the earth.[27] In 1900 Willie Boy resided near whites and was exercising care over other Indians, living in accordance with the teachings both of Chemehuevi culture and of Wovoka.

Willie Boy appeared again in white records around 1905, when he was arrested in Victorville and sent to San Bernardino, where he served a sentence in the county jail variously given at from twenty to forty days. Since the arrest records are no longer extant, we have only the press coverage of the time and the more recent comments in the newsletter of the sheriff's association to try to determine the charge.

During the manhunt the Victorville incident surfaced about the time of Ben de Crevecoeur's "discovery" of the liquor that allegedly preceded William Mike's death, and so the early charge became disturbing the peace associated with drunkenness.[28] But a later sheriff's version described the incident as unruliness following a baseball game in which Willie Boy had hit a home run and made no reference to alcohol.[29] What is clear is that he served time. A photograph of the era shows him in a striped jail suit, wearing number 674 (see fig. 5). Sometime after this incident, Willie Boy and some of his family, apparently including the orphans, moved to Twentynine Palms, where the Mikes and Bonifaces also lived.

When Willie Boy could choose to pose for a photograph, as he did in Banning in September 1909, just before the incident, his dress is revealing. As can be seen, he is wearing a hat with a pronounced brim, a white shirt and necktie, the shirt complemented by sleeve garters (see fig. 6). He is dressed in the dapper fashion of the day. Compare Willie Boy's image in 1909 with that of Wovoka, the Ghost Dance prophet, in 1892.

After much effort, ethnographer James Mooney finally got Wovoka to agree to be photographed. Mooney wrote at the time: "He believed that it was better for the Indians to follow the white man's road and to adopt the habits of civilization. If appearances are in evidence he is sincere in this, for he was dressed in a good suit of white man's clothing, and works regularly on a ranch. . . . he got ready for the operation by knotting a handkerchief about his neck, fastening an eagle feather at his right elbow, and taking a wide brim sombrero upon his knee" (see fig. 7).[30]

It appears that contemporary press accounts, and some written later, which took Willie Boy's 1909 photograph as evidence of acculturation, missed the mark. Like Wovoka, Willie Boy's fashionable attire did not mean abandonment of his Indian culture or his wholesale embracing of white ways. Willie Boy and Wovoka could dress well, according to white standards, without losing their Indian identity. Willie Boy's dress for that photograph, however, may provide insight into the role of the Ghost Dance prophet in his own life.

Fig. 6. Photograph of Willie Boy in Banning before incident, 1909 (Courtesy of Special Collections, Rivera Library, University of California, Riverside)

Fig. 7. Photograph of Wovoka, source of the 1890 Ghost Dance revival (Courtesy of The Smithsonian Institution, Photo No. 1659-A)

" 'Love is hard.' That's what she said." Alberta looked at us directly. "When Adrian said you were coming, I thought and thought about what my mother used to say about this business, and last night it came back to me. She would shake her head and say, 'Love is hard.' What she meant was that love should never have

happened. Never. They were too close. It isn't like that anymore, but it was then. People knew who you were."

"That's right," Adrian added. "People back then kept track of who were your relatives, who you could and could not marry. It seems strange now, we're all so intermingled."

"Yeah, it could never happen now, not since maybe the thirties or forties," added Alberta. "We're way too mixed now for that."

"They tried to do what was not right, what they should not have done," Alberta continued. "They knew. She knew. He knew. They wanted it, but the families couldn't let it happen. She went with him once before you know, and members of both families went to get them and bring them back. If they had stayed together, both families would have to cut them off. She wanted him. She wanted her way. He wanted his way. There had to be trouble, but the families didn't want it."

What happened to Willie Boy's sister, Georgia Bruce? Who knows? What was Willie Boy's last name. Alberta said she did not know and never asked her mother; the family all called him Willie Boy. Much to our surprise, she suddenly recalled Willie Boy's mother's Indian name. "It sounds," said Adrian," like 'So Iris.'"

"Yes, that's pretty close," responded Alberta. "I don't remember her English name, but Mary Lou will—she lived with Mary Lou for a while."

We asked Alberta one further question before leaving. Did she know that Segundo Chino had later married William Mike's widow, Maria? "Oh yeah," Alberta said. "The widow got to know him from the chase. But he had been around before. He went to bring Willie Boy back the first time; it was his duty. He was from our family." You mean Chino was Willie Boy's relative? "Yes, of course." We thought he was a Serrano. "No, Chemehuevi."

*Mary Lou Brown, in her early eighties, consented
to talk to us in her home. Adrian, who had arranged
the meeting, accompanied us. Mary Lou had been
married to William Waco, a first cousin of Willie
Boy's. In the 1930s, Mary Snyder, Willie Boy's mother,
came to live with Mary Lou and her husband for a
while in Parker before Mary Snyder got her own place.
Mary Snyder "was a wonderful basket maker, her
[identifying] sign was the beetle, sometimes the rattlesnake. Some of her baskets are in the museum."*

*"The old people didn't tell me much, didn't tell
anybody much, and now I wish they had. Mary Snyder
came here a few years after her son died in Nevada, in
a sanatorium, in 1927 or 1928. She was very nice. . . .
They did what was wrong. Sometimes young people
are like that; they want what they want. But they were
too close, first cousins, I think,[31] and it could not be
permitted. The girl wanted it as much as he did. He
didn't die from the posse. How could they catch him?
He ran like the wind. They killed an animal and
burned it, or something like that.*

*"Willie Boy came to Mr. Mike, I think it was behind
a shed, and they argued. But Willie Boy brought a
gun. He never should have killed Mr. Mike 'cause
there was no going back then, not like before. Well,
there's no point going into all of this because, after
all, they are gone, and we don't talk, we just don't talk
about this once its over. But it should be told now.
Adrian agreed. So I talk to you now."*

William Mike had strong feelings about his daughter Carlota. He told Clara True that he disapproved of
a marriage between her and Willie Boy because she
was too young and Willie Boy already had a wife.[32]
But these were remarks designed to appease white
curiosity and deflect attention from his real thoughts.

By 1909 Carlota was at least sixteen, no longer a girl but a young woman capable of raising a family. An objection based upon age may have appealed to white sensibilities and prepared the way for later erroneous reporting of her age as fourteen. But to Chemehuevis, to be fifteen or sixteen qualified a young woman for marriage.[33] Willie Boy's existing marriage could have been easily dissolved. Carobeth Harrington caused George Laird to dissolve his marriage to his wife, Annie, in favor of her, an action that either Chemehuevi party could initiate at will to terminate a liaison.[34]

William Mike's real objections, then, were somewhat different from the reasons he gave to the Indian agent. According to his family's lore, William Mike genuinely disliked Willie Boy and wanted his daughter to have nothing to do with him.[35] William Mike's objection stemmed from a distant family relationship between Willie Boy and Carlota,[36] a situation that in 1909 George Laird insisted meant "that marriage between siblings or cousins was absolutely forbidden."[37]

Some months before the September 26, 1909 incident, however, Willie Boy and Carlota had left the reservation at Twentynine Palms and stayed out all night together. Mike and Willie Boy family members found them and brought Carlota back. Upon her return, she stayed briefly in the house of Jim Pine, the "chief" (or more likely *capitan*) of that reservation. Her stay provided time for tempers to cool. Clara True thought that Willie Boy had taken her in revenge for the stealing of one of his kinswomen by a member of the Mike clan.[38] If that was the only reason, why did he persist in his desire to marry her? Furthermore, Clara knew nothing of Carlota's desires.

As a runner, Willie Boy would have had some vestigial shamanistic power and status among the Indians at Twentynine Palms. William Mike also was a shaman in his own right,[39] a powerfully built man of great physical strength and spiritual authority. William Mike had once tried to get Clara True to file a claim on a mountain on his behalf, since, as an Indian, he could not do so before white law. He told Clara True that he had found a secret gold mine there and wanted to protect it against white intrusion.[40] What seems more likely is that the mountain was sacred to him and he wanted to protect it for spiritual purposes.[41]

The conflict between William Mike and Willie Boy over Mike's daughter came down to a contest of wills and spiritual power between a shaman and a runner. We see this as not just a generational conflict between the twenty-eight-year-old Willie Boy and the sixty-five-year-old William Mike but also a conflict between the new ways of the Ghost Dance revival and the ancient Chemehuevi ways, which had rejected the Ghost Dance. Willie Boy's desire to marry William Mike's daughter, and her desire to be with him even at the cost of breaking tribal taboo, can be seen as an attempt to combine elements of the past with the promise of the new in a future they thought would be better. Both were willing to violate tribal standards, but Willie Boy was willing to use force to get his way.

That night, as we drove back toward Twentynine Palms, we talked animatedly about the day's events. While we tried to see the numinous land and think of it as it might have appeared to the Chemehuevi of eighty years ago, we could not; our Christianized eyes did not permit it.

Alberta told us of an incident that illustrated for her why we should pursue this inquiry. When the film Tell Them Willie Boy Is Here *came to Parker, a male cousin of Adrian's took Alberta's mother and aunt to the drive-in to see it. He sat in the front while the two women sat in back. He found the experience totally confusing. As soon as the film started, the women began to talk. "That's not right, nobody did that, that's wrong. . . . How come there's no Chemehuevis in this? What are they talking? That's not Chemehuevi and it sure isn't Paiute or Mojave. What is it?" These Chemehuevi women were displeased. We said we thought the language was Cahuilla because Catherine Saubel of Morongo played Maria Mike. "See," said Adrian, "it's time." The Chemehuevi were ready to tell their view of the incident. Joe and Adrian permitted and facilitated our inquiry among other Chemehuevis so that this story could become part of what they call history, even if it is white history.*

Lawton knew of the taboo, of Willie Boy and Carlota's being related, and of a previous incident of alleged abduction, all of which he mentions on page 10 of his novel. These same pieces of information are related in the film *Tell Them Willie Boy Is Here*. In each case, however, the information is not presented as significant, and it is distorted in important ways from the Chemehuevi tradition.

What are the significant discrepancies, and what do they mean? First, the notion that Willie Boy kidnapped Carlota earlier reinforces the 1909 act as a kidnap. Absent from this view is any sense of Carlota's own agency and responsibility in her relationship with Willie Boy. In the white version Willie Boy is the sole important actor; the man, not the woman, makes the decisions. Carlota is a victim.

Second, this lack of mutuality between the oppositely attracted sexes is further underscored by a lack of mutuality between the different families to try to resolve the crisis of taboo violation. In Lawton's version the father, carrying a rifle, tracks down the errant couple, threatens Willie Boy at gunpoint, and brings his daughter back. No mention is made of families, only of individuals, and Willie Boy is treated as a loner.

Third, and most important, while much of the information about the Chemehuevi was available to the white storyteller, the information could not be used to explain something alternative to the dominant tale. The information has been viewed through an ethnocentric lens and rendered inert because a Chemehuevi context has not been considered significant.

Our fieldwork among the Chemehuevi and research into published ethnography reveals Willie Boy's background as a runner, the influence of the Ghost Dance upon him, Carlota's role as an actor in the story, the conflict between individual and family desires versus tribal taboo, and the centrality of love in the story. Before we offer our version of the tale, we present a telling in the Chemehuevi style in the next chapter.

7

A
Simple Story
Retold

This chapter could strike the reader as oddly brief, but it constitutes a way to illustrate what Calvin Martin was getting at in differentiating between what he called biological and anthropological time. Mrs. Mary Lou Brown told us, when speaking of the Willie Boy tale, "This is a simple story, easily told." From a Chemehuevi perspective, the tale is brief and Indian focused. In that spirit, we have attempted to retell the episode in the pattern of Chemehuevi storytelling recounted by Carobeth Laird. She was the first white person to put Chemehuevi myth into both English and printed format as a necessary first step in bringing Chemehuevi lore to a wider audience. A Chemehuevi story of Willie Boy has not been written before. We offer this Chemehuevi oral version of Willie Boy, reduced to print, to create a text. In the next chapter we will bring this text into dialogue with the white text to try to produce an inclusive history of the event.

Whenever my mother would tell this story, she always began by saying, "Love is hard."

Willie Boy lived with his mother in the desert. She was a wonderful basket maker, and her sign was the rattlesnake. She made her baskets without fear that the snake would strike her. Willie Boy was a very good hunter because he could run faster than many animals. He needed a wife, but there were no young women nearby. He was young and strong, so he went across the desert looking for a wife. One day he saw his cousin, Carlota, and he wanted her. She looked back at him openly, and they both ran away together. Family [members] followed and found them. Willie Boy and Carlota were separated. He was not to look at her again. Both their hearts were still restless. He wanted Carlota, but her father was a man of power. One night Willie Boy got a rifle and came to see her father. They argued, and Willie Boy got mad. Willie Boy killed her father, then he and Carlota ran away again.

This time the whites chased them, along with some of The People. Willie Boy hid his wife in a wash, gave her his coat and waterskin, and went for food. He ran in the old way, for he was like the wind, and no one could catch him then. He came back with food but could not find his wife. He searched everywhere, but she had died. He found the men chasing him and shot their horses with his rifle so that they would have to run like he did. They could not. He was so much faster that he quickly ran off.

In his running he came again to his mother, but she now turned away. He ran further, far out into the desert, away from all his family. None of The People saw him again, and we later heard that he had died.

113

8

How Willie Boy Recovered His Song

Desert bibliographer E. I. Edwards once told the prevailing Willie Boy story in one hundred words:

"Willie Boy—a young Indian—gulped too much firewater, murdered his sweetheart's father in Banning town, kidnapped the girl and attempted escape on foot across rugged desert country. As the pursuing posse drew near, he murdered his sweetheart because she impeded his progress. Later, he shot and wounded one of the posse. Eventually they came upon him, only to find that he had removed a shoe, applied his toe to the rifle, and—with his last remaining bullet—triggered his soul into eternity. Following early Indian custom—and perhaps with an eye toward convenience—they cremated his bloated, sun-parched body.[1]

We now tell our version of the Willie Boy episode,

trying to bring together the verifiable elements in the story from Chemehuevi and white perspectives. The conventional story begins in Banning. We know, however, that it began months earlier, in late 1908 or early 1909, in Twentynine Palms, when Willie Boy and his cousin Carlota ran away. The families of the would-be lovers sought to prevent their becoming husband and wife and so pursued them. When caught, Willie Boy and Carlota were separated. She was sent to the house of Jim Pine, a Serrano and a neutral in the Chemehuevi conflict, where she stayed overnight until tempers cooled. Some months afterward her family migrated to Banning to work the fruit harvest. Willie Boy followed later.

We now come to the night of September 26, 1909, and the issue of alcohol. Why would Willie Boy challenge a shaman for his daughter after drinking? Since this was his second attempt to marry her, Willie Boy thought he needed additional power for the confrontation and took from whites the advantage of a rifle. That behavior was consistent with Wovoka's message; contemplating violence against another Indian was not.

Drinking beforehand makes no sense except in the ethnocentric worldview in which Indians have to find courage in a bottle before attempting a difficult task. Drinking violated Wovoka's teachings. Willie Boy's prior reputation as a hard-working and nondrinking person was dismissed as soon as Ben de Crevecoeur came up with the liquor story. Rumor alone has convicted Willie Boy of drinking before approaching the Mike camp. Yet the ethnographic background we have reconstructed about him argues against it. We have concluded, therefore, that Willie Boy was sober when he approached the Mike family that night.

What happened under the trees at the Gilman Ranch cannot be accurately determined. According to both the Mike and Willie Boy family traditions, the two men first argued. This may not have been a quarrel with raised voices, but it would have been no less serious or intense.[2] After William Mike had been killed, his wife, Maria, unsuccessfully tried to wrest the rifle from Willie Boy and then urged her daughter to accompany him to spare the rest of the family his revenge.[3] Carlota joined him because she wanted to and also to protect her family.

An argument before the shooting seems right. Even the coroner wrote it up as a "gunshot wound in left eye inflicted by Willie Boy with intent to commit murder,"[4] an allegation implying intent imposed after the fact. For Willie Boy to have killed William Mike deliberately, while the shaman slept, would have been cowardly and would have still left unresolved the issues of respective power and determination of the future. A deliberate murder would compound further the seriousness of the violation of tribal taboo against cousins' marrying.

For Willie Boy to have spared the remainder of the Mike family then at the ranch suggests a willingness to turn away from the blood feud and revenge-seeking for which the Chemehuevi had been noted. Regardless of his subsequent treatment of the Mike family, Willie Boy had gone to their camp to have his way and had brought a rifle to ensure he got it. Whether he murdered William Mike or whether the shaman died in a struggle over the weapon, Willie Boy initiated the events. After killing William Mike, Willie Boy and Carlota left together.

THE MIKE FAMILY, THE TRACKERS, AND THE POSSE

Immediately after Willie Boy killed William Mike and left with his daughter, Carlota, Maria and her remaining children fled into the foothills above Banning. Maria feared that Willie Boy might change his mind, return, and kill them all according to Chemehuevi custom.[5] In the interval variously given as from nine to twelve hours between William Mike's death and the notification of authorities, Maria came to a plan of action. Since the death occurred off a reservation, she would have to resort to the care of friends and strangers for prosecution of her husband's killer.

Whether Maria conferred with other than her family cannot be known, but she decided to contact the Indian and white police. She further decided that none of the male members of the Mike family would participate in the hunt. The intervening time Maria gave Willie Boy and Carlota allowed them a chance to flee; invoking the authorities gave Maria a power with which to combat Willie Boy's potential return, protect her remaining family, and possibly get Carlota returned.

Maria also may have had deeper, more conflicting motives for her decision. An older source of Mike family tradition holds that Maria approved of Willie Boy's suit for Carlota and that Maria encouraged it.[6] If true, then Maria would have been acting against the wishes of William Mike, her husband. Once William Mike was dead, she may have felt remorse and decided to pursue the Chemehuevi tradition of revenge, not by using her family members, but by seeking outside help.

Maria's allies among the Indian police would be critical. Any posse would have to be joint Indian and white, and while whites enjoyed bragging about their tracking abilities, the proper Indian trackers accompanying them could shorten a chase while permitting whites to take the credit. William Mike had been well liked around Banning by whites and by many of the Indians on the Morongo Reservation located there.

The two primary Indian policemen who helped Maria were John Hyde and Segundo Chino. Hyde was a Yaqui, a group with a reputation as guerrilla fighters, and he was in his late twenties and in sufficiently good physical condition to be considered able to pursue Willie Boy at a reasonable pace. Chino, listed on the register as a Serrano, at forty-eight was too old for fast tracking, but he knew the terrain extremely well and was a senior policeman at Morongo.[7] Chino was also part-Chemehuevi, a member of Willie Boy's family, and one of those who had helped separate the couple when they had run away the first time.[8] These men would lead and inform the white posse about the couple's flight.

Their role in spurring the posse to continue cannot be overestimated. They provided the information that Carlota had apparently cut herself, perhaps on cactus, which the press exaggerated into bloody footprints on the sand.[9] They supposedly found the signs that she had been sexually violated, which the posse and press repeated. If it seemed to the Mike family that the posse did "more camping than chasing,"[10] the pursuit that was made was largely fueled by the Indian tracker reports, exaggerated or distorted by white possemen or the press, which in turn spurred public sympathy for Carlota and the quest to bring Willie Boy to justice.

In helping to incite white anger against Willie Boy, Chino and Hyde nevertheless risked intensifying white hatred against the Indians at Morongo. They undertook such a risk because of the power of their enemy. Willie Boy was a runner with a rifle who had twice defied tribal taboo and then broken Chemehuevi and white law in killing William Mike. Using whites now to settle a tribal matter increased their power while counteracting Willie Boy's.

One of the more blatant examples of manipulation of whites by Indians involved the written message of Carlota indicating that she was growing weary and soon would die. The Indian trackers supposedly discovered this written message and translated it for the posse and press. Clara True, who communicated with the Chemehuevi in Spanish because she did not know their language, had not known that these Indians had written communication and promised to compare this inscription with petroglyphs in the desert to see if she could learn this written language.[11] Nothing ever came of it because there was nothing to it. This story, however, added to the drama of the chase and forced the posse to continue, overcoming the desire to quit.

Indian manipulation of whites to settle a personal score went awry in The Pipes. Hyde, far ahead of the rest of the posse, found Carlota's body lying face down. The circumstantial evidence argues that he, not Willie Boy, killed her. The bullet had, according to coroner Dickson, struck her "just behind the left shoulder . . . cutting its way downward through her breast and coming out through the right abdominal cavity,"[12] a wound consistent with the trajectory of a long-range shot. A falling bullet hit her high in the back and exited low. If Willie Boy had done it, the shot would have been straight, fired at close range, and the bullet's path through her body would have been direct.

We think we can reconstruct what Hyde saw coming up The Pipes that morning. Given the time of day in the high desert, prior to 7:00 A.M., it was chilly, with the temperature at about 50 degrees Fahrenheit.[13] Ahead of him at perhaps seventy-five or one hundred yards, a figure moved though the rocks carrying a canteen and wearing, or carrying, a coat. Carlota was dark complected, had black hair, stood 5'6" tall and weighed 130 pounds. Willie Boy was two inches taller and twenty pounds heavier, differences not noticeable at such a distance. Hyde undoubtedly thought that he had come upon Willie Boy and fired. But when the tracker came upon the body, it was not Willie Boy but Carlota. Reche got the credit for the discovery, and Willie Boy got the blame for her death.

Even the coroner and his jury had misgivings about Willie Boy's guilt. In his official report coroner Dickson recorded her cause of death as "gunshot wound in back fired by party to the [coroner's] jury unknown."[14]

The verdict is all the more remarkable, since one of the jurors, Joe Knowlin, was a posseman. The jury report suggests that the posse suspected a tragedy in Carlota's death but did not wish to alienate the Indian trackers with a more probing inquiry. In effect, the ambiguous finding allowed the press to convict Willie Boy of her murder.[15]

RUBY MOUNTAIN

In The Pipes, Willie Boy had left Carlota with what remained of their possessions and his coat while he set out for more supplies. According to the lore of both the Mike and Willie Boy families, the young man loved Carlota and would not have killed her. In time of conflict a warrior would have hid his wife, gone for help, and then returned. His tracks in flight replicated those of the runner seen by Chemehuevi youths who earlier had tried to follow their runner friend. Willie Boy ran in the Chemehuevi way of the runner. He ran for aid, not to flee. And he came back to the area when he had reprovisioned himself.

The tale that some old woman at Twentynine Palms had thrown away his rifle and ammunition is a fable, unsupported by evidence. Clara True observed that the residents of the oasis, all of whom were Indian, had been taken into protective custody by Sheriff Ralphs and brought to Banning for their safety. Unbeknownst to Clara or other whites, Willie Boy's mother was among them, picked up by the posse that Randolph Madison accompanied.[16] Clara further noted that some of Willie Boy's family at Twentynine Palms fled quickly into the desert following news of William

Mike's death, and she was convinced that they had resupplied Willie Boy during the chase.[17]

With new supplies, Willie Boy and Carlota could have continued their flight. Willie Boy's return toward The Pipes, however, became interrupted near Bullion, later Ruby Mountain, when he discovered the posse. He needed to draw attention to himself and away from her hiding place. The ambush hardly constituted the merciless attack that has been customarily portrayed. The possemen were dismounted, moving among the rocks, and Willie Boy shot first at their horses. He was already more than a match for them mounted; on foot they could not have kept his pace nor, probably, Carlota's.

Reche's wound probably came from Willie Boy firing at the gleam of sun on metal, since Reche wore his handcuffs on his hip (see fig. 2 above). A man scrambling around the rocks carrying that type of reflector would have drawn fire. Ironically, Hyde, who had found Carlota's body, ran for aid for Reche. Hyde reported that words had been exchanged between Willie Boy and the possemen even before he left. Hyde said Willie Boy had shouted down to them that he would not kill a white man, only Indians; further insults and comments continued. We think it likely that in this exchange Willie Boy learned that she was dead and that that fact shaped his words.

Their mutual desire resulted in all the pain they had caused themselves and their respective families. At Ruby Mountain, Willie Boy learned that Carlota—the reason for his confrontation with the shaman William Mike, for defying Chemehuevi taboo and bearing the price of ostracism from both families, for running away to create a new life—no longer existed in this world.

There was no reason to surrender. Willie Boy could have run away easily. Looking down at the ambush site from his perspective (see fig. 8), it is obvious he had the posse trapped, not the reverse. Since he had already outrun mounted possemen, dismounted men without horses and with a comrade to care for would have been no obstacle to his escape. Moreover, surrender would have meant placing himself under the judgment of white law and/or Mike family revenge.

Both Willie Boy and the possemen waited for darkness to envelope Ruby Mountain but for very different reasons. According to the Ghost Dance teachings, a follower had the greatest opportunity to see and communicate with the dead at night, when their spirits were active in this world. The best time to join them would be before dawn because they disappeared during the day.[18] The posse wanted darkness to extract Reche and take him to a doctor for treatment. Willie Boy used the darkness to join Carlota by killing himself with the rifle. Since he had other supplies (see fig. 9), there is no reason to think that he used his last cartridge for this act. Later, when the posse found his body, nobody wanted to check the pockets of a rotting corpse to determine if he had more ammunition.

The ambush at Ruby Mountain was not the effort of a desperate man, run to the ground by the posse, to stage a final shoot-out with his pursuers. Press claims that the posse had Willie Boy surrounded should be corrected to read that he was "surrounded" on only

123

Fig. 8. Photograph of Ruby Mountain ambush site from Willie Boy's view (Photo by Tom Morr)

Fig. 9. Photograph of food tins found at Willie Boy ambush site, ca. 1958 (Courtesy of Special Collections, Rivera Library, University of California, Riverside)

one side. The ambush was the diversionary tactic of a reprovisioned runner to deflect attention from his reunion with his beloved. In our opinion he did not choose to commit suicide because the posse wore him out; he killed himself to rejoin Carlota. If Willie Boy was desperate at Ruby Mountain, the cause was love.

REPERCUSSIONS
Neither white nor Indian culture could accept Willie Boy's suicide. Local lawmen in Riverside and San Bernardino counties used the manhunt as proof of their effectiveness as peace officers, securing appointment or reelection at the time and continuing to invoke the incident throughout their careers. Erecting a monument to law enforcement on Ruby Mountain in 1966 further exemplified the process and revealed how the continuing lens of Indian-hating—ethnocentrism modified by cultural myth—refracts human

experience into something it was not. The monument ignored the suicide and affirmed that the posse had done its job; the continuing Mother's Day celebration of the posse at Landers, California, reaffirms the dominant story.

Even the well meaning proved limited in their vision by unquestioned ethnocentric assumptions. Randolph Madison, the reporter who accompanied the last posse to claim Willie Boy's body, thought that in death Willie Boy had returned to his Indian ways, renouncing the world of the whites. White liquor caused his reversion to Indian barbarism, and the white rifle finally made him "a good Indian."

Madison took the photographs and wrote much of the prose associated with this final outing, and he is the one who defined the "return to Indian custom" theme, which quickly became "reversion to Indian barbarism."[19] Willie Boy came to represent a deviation from the road toward white "civilization" that many thought he was pursuing and a return to Indian "savagery." (See the Appendix for the writers who have invoked this theme.) Complementing this approach was the emphasis by Madison and other members of the press at the time, followed by subsequent authors, of focusing on Willie Boy's lust ("reversion"), which meant their ignoring the issue of love. The tragedy inherent in the story went unacknowledged.

Intrinsic to the idea of reversion was the concept that Indians, or at least the "good" ones, were assimilating to white ways; the more they acted like whites, the better and more civilized they became. Under the influence of Indian-hating, there was no way intellectually for most whites to comprehend, even if they knew of it, an Indian culture like the Chemehuevi in which cultural borrowing, whether from Indians or whites, meant no loss of Chemehuevi culture.[20] Cultural borrowing did not mean cultural replacement. Willie Boy did not *revert* to his Chemehuevi culture from September 26 to October 7, 1909; he *practiced* it, modified in accordance with the teachings of Wovoka.

To Chemehuevis in his own and the Mike family, Willie Boy did not die. He was a runner, he could escape, and so he did. Willie Boy and Carlota had become anathema to their families, a source of great pain, and so would not have been discussed after the incident. In Chemehuevi culture of that time, it was taboo to mention or speak the name of the dead.[21] Added to that fact was the fear that, if Willie Boy was still alive, to speak of him would invite his revenge. Immediately after the manhunt the Chemehuevi of Twentynine Palms abandoned their permanent settlement there, and it is still not regularly occupied by them today.[22]

"Out by Needles, in the desert, the Mojave have this maze," Adrian, who is Chemehuevi-Mojave told us. "It's about as high as a man and has lots of twists and turns, real sharp. You run it when you're troubled, when you have real problems. You're supposed to run through it as fast as you can without looking back, and each turn, each elbow, is so tight and narrow that the evil spirits that are following you will get caught there. When you leave the maze, the bad spirits stay behind, trapped, and you're free."

How Willie Boy Recovered His Song

9

Conclusion

"When Anglo-Americans look across the Mexican border or into an Indian reservation, they are more likely to see stereotypes than recognizable individuals or particular groups," writes historian Patricia Nelson Limerick.

The same distortion of vision no doubt works the other way too. The unitary character known as "the white man" has never existed, nor has "the Indian." Yet the phrases receive constant use, as if they carried necessary meaning. Indians, Hispanics, Asians, blacks, Anglos, businesspeople, workers, politicians, bureaucrats, natives, and newcomers, we share the same region and its history, but we wait to be introduced. The serious exploration of the historical process that made us neighbors provides that introduction.[1]

In the case of native peoples, however, Indian-hating frequently prevents that introduction.

In the historical development of the Willie Boy incident, we can see illustrated Melville's metaphysics of Indian-hating. The climate of Indian-hating in Banning in 1909 stemmed from the friction between whites and Indians over reservation land claimed by the predominantly Cahuilla and Serrano living on the Morongo Reservation. Neither Willie Boy nor the Mike family lived at Morongo; neither were they Cahuilla or Serrano. Yet the killing of one non-Morongo Indian by another, even though or possibly because it happened off the reservation, provided a target against which whites could vent their anger.

Melville observed that, in addition to the prevailing anti-Indian sentiment of the local community, the Indian-hater par excellence has his own private grievance, real or imagined, to add to the general antipathy. While many of the white possemen fit the description of Indian-hater par excellence because poor whites competed directly with poor Indians for land around Banning, the most remarkable proved to be Ben de Crevecoeur. As a young boy, he and his family had been dispossessed by federal marshals for squatting on land claimed by the Morongo Reservation.

With the killing of William Mike, de Crevecoeur had an opportunity to strike out at an Indian directly, even though Willie Boy was not one of the Indians responsible for the de Crevecoeur family's trouble. Late in the Willie Boy episode Ben de Crevecoeur came up with the story that Willie Boy had been drinking before going to William Mike's camp; Ben de Crevecoeur showed reporter Randolph Madison the "writing" that a supposedly abused and desperate Carlota had left in the sand; and Ben de Crevecoeur told Madison about the alleged Paiute customs of bride kidnap and of cremation.

De Crevecoeur figured prominently in retelling the story, adding to its Indian-hating message. He claimed that the possemen could hear Carlota's sobs but could not close the pursuit and help her; he increased Willie Boy's alleged liquor consumption from the original two bottles of whiskey and one of beer to half a suitcase full; he redrew Carlota's "written message" for a 1941 article; and he called Willie Boy a bad Indian, one who went sour by failing to adhere to white ways.

This final theme—that Willie Boy had reverted to savagery—initiated by the press at the time and reiterated by subsequent writers, most clearly exemplifies Melville's point about the Indian-hater par excellence: nothing that Indians do can ever qualify them for acceptance or trust by the "civilized." Willie Boy's killing of William Mike was based in neither Chemehuevi nor white culture; rather, it stemmed from human passion. Yet that passion, coupled with the grossly erroneous charge of bride kidnapping, actually brought Indian-hating to an interpretive level that made the story plausible as an example of justice in the Old West. Obviously, that story of justice had to be told at the expense of the real Indians who lived it.

Ben de Crevecoeur's Indian-hating reached far beyond himself and his community. The local impact can be seen in the tragedy of Joe Toutain, who waited nearly fifty years to reveal his friendship and admiration for Willie Boy, remaining silent all those years because of the anger Banning people felt toward Willie Boy and reinforced by de Crevecoeur. Harry Lawton thought to discount some of "Ben's hokum" in dismissing Carlota's written message. Lawton accepted that same "hokum," however, when he uncritically took both Madison's stories about Paiute customs and the curious confession of Otto Sweeters. Through Lawton, de Crevecoeur's stories also influenced Polonsky and the film *Tell Them Willie Boy Is Here.*

Through both the novel and the film, Ben de Crevecoeur sucked the Cahuilla at Morongo Reservation into the vortex of his Indian-hating. Jane Penn, a member of one of the first Cahuilla families at Morongo and an activist, promoted an awareness of Indian history and contemporary Indian problems at the reservation on which she had been born in 1910.[2] The Willie Boy episode had occurred shortly before her birth, and it was a subject in which she took an interest. We have already noted her friendship with Lawton and the importance of filming on the reservation for the Cahuilla economy. Lawton helped in fundraising for the Malki Museum at Morongo Reservation, which was Jane Penn's creation; she authorized the press at Malki to reprint Lawton's novel, an ongoing activity that began in 1976. Through Cahuilla endorsement of the novel and participation in the film *Tell Them Willie Boy Is Here,* native peoples sadly have been drawn into Indian-hating. Neither Lawton nor Penn nor Polonsky were Indian-haters, but they accepted the views of an Indian-hater in their interpretations of Willie Boy. As Roy Harvey Pearce observed, "We must learn to take Indian-hating with high seriousness. We must learn at once to respect and fear it."[3]

The prevailing story of Willie Boy has held its ground, thanks to the skillful writing of Harry Lawton and the brooding film of Abraham Polonsky. As a journalist writing a novel, Lawton's concern was to tell the story from a single, focused perspective, to bring his reader into the narrative and keep the reader in his grasp. Writing fiction is not writing history, and once a historical episode has been enveloped in a novelist's tale, it is very, very difficult to recover it for the discipline.

A film made from a novelist's account pushes the tale ever further from the reality that, in this instance, Lawton as journalist thought he was portraying. Polonsky reversed Lawton's praise of the posse, and Lawton pronounced himself satisfied with the transformation. Both the novel and the film claimed to be relating historical fact, but as Jon Tuska noted, in making films about history, American directors have not respected accuracy. Hence film can be even more problematic to analyze than its sources.[4]

For historians, the methodological problems to be dealt with in claiming this story for the discipline have been extremely difficult. From the perspective of what had been recorded, we had to overcome not only the problems of racism, gender bias, and ethnocentrism in newspapers and magazines but also the manipulation of Indians by whites for political purposes. For some writers, tangents and digressions have deflected attention away from the true subject of the tale. Thus Taft's visit, the Indian uprising, the suitcase full of whiskey, bride kidnapping, Billy Boy/Paiute, beating the old woman at Twentynine Palms, and many other distractions have had to be carefully investigated before the incident could be analyzed on its own terms.

Determining the names of the Indian protagonists, along with their correct tribal identities, proved to be only the beginning of our inquiry into an Indian perspective. We had to gain some degree of acceptance by Indians for them to talk to us. We realize that we have come together for different purposes in this mutual exploration of the Indian-white past.

We had to identify the more subtle, as well as blatant, impact that ethnocentrism and gender bias can have on any inquiry. We knew that we needed to determine whether an Indian woman's perspective on these events could be ascertained, but we were unprepared for what we found. We may have unconsciously begun by accepting Willie Boy's role as the exclusive actor; we may also have not questioned hard enough at the outset the notion of Indian as victim.

Getting at the Chemehuevi story was difficult because of ignorance. The ethnographic work available was scant and needed to be supplemented with interview fieldwork. Once we found the right people, the Chemehuevi were most generous with their time and gracious in tolerating our questions.

Our ethnographic work has enabled us to reconstruct a historical ethnography that illuminates this story as nothing else could. We have presented our fieldwork as an interaction with Chemehuevis, an interaction in which they have power. The combination of ethnography with historical documents—ethnohistory—has provided a cultural context for behavior that has eluded earlier tellers of the tale. The frontier myth in American history, what Richard Drinnon has called "the metaphysics of Indian-hating and empire building,"[5] has shaped this story into the triumph of "civilization over savagery." By identifying the power of that myth and showing how it affected portrayals of Willie Boy, the Indian can be freed from a white storytelling dominated exclusively by Indian-hating.

Simultaneously, by showing the power of the Ghost Dance in Chemehuevi life, we can see a culture undergoing historic change. Willie Boy's song is part of the Ghost Dance, of cultural renewal that Wovoka preached and that many Chemehuevi rejected. By identifying the power of that renewal, we can see Willie Boy's behavior in a different light. His attempt to affirm a new way broke with traditional values. Within the Chemehuevi cultural complex, Willie Boy and Carlota's story emerges as a tragedy.

In this book we have presented an approach that might be useful for including previously excluded peoples from the history of the United States. In chapters 2 through 7 we have examined the various representations of Willie Boy in popular culture, analyzed historical documents, and presented the results of ethnographic fieldwork and research, all of which was necessary to create a historical ethnography, before we could advance another retelling. Chapter 8, then, constitutes the hypothesis of "pragmatic hermeneutics" discussed in the Introduction. We offer this approach as a way to move beyond the impasse in writing about Indian-white contact and as a provisional vehicle for telling the story of those preliterate groups whom Eric Wolf called "the people without history."[6] Five centuries after Columbus's landfall, historians cannot afford to leave native peoples out of the story they share with whites.

135

Appendix

Willie Boy: Published Accounts

We list here in chronological order the thirty-four published accounts of the Willie Boy story known to us. The first line of each entry includes a listing of themes, identified by the following abbreviations:

A/D	Alcohol/drunkenness	OW	Old woman beaten
BK	Bride kidnapping	PA	Previous abduction or
DS	Denied her schooling		affront
IU	Indian uprising	PF	Paiute funeral
KW	Killed white man	RS	Return to savagery
	earlier	SB	San Bernardino
MG	Murdered girl	TV	Taft visit
MS	Old Mike sleeping	WB	Willie Boy
ND	WB did not die	WL	Written Indian
			language

In the description of the items, (L) indicates an account that draws heavily or exclusively upon Lawton's so-called nonfiction novel (no. 11).

1. Paul   MG

    Nina Howard Paul, "The Purple Boundary,"
    Sunset Magazine (September, 1926), pp 24–
    26, 57–64.

    Fiction. Heroine captures Squint Lopez. (see no.
    12.)

2. Wood   MG, MS, PA, PF, RS, WL

    Willard S. Wood, "Bad Indian in the Moron-
    gos," *Westways* (April, 1935), pp 10–11, 34.

    Non-fiction. Sources: Ben and Wal de Creve-
    coeur, Charlie Reche, Joe Toutain. Ben is
    primary.

3. Hughes   A/D, MG, MS, PA, PF, WL

    Tom Hughes, *History of Banning and San Gor-
    gonio Pass.* Banning: Banning Record Print,
    1939, pp 173–174.

    Non-fiction. Sources: "Ben and Wally de Creve-
    coeur, Joe Waite, and E. C. Brock, all mem-
    bers of the pursuing posse. Previous accounts
    of his having caused the disappearances of a
    prospector or prior Indian wives seem to have
    been fastened upon him out of pure gener-
    osity." (173)

4. Carling   A/D, IU, MG, MS, PA, PF, RS, WL

    James L. Carling, "On the Trail of Willie Boy,"
    The Desert Magazine (November, 1941), pp 6–11.

    Non-fiction. Sources: Toutain "but it was from
    Ben de Crevecoeur that I got the complete
    story."(6) Quotes Ben about a white boy friend
    of WB's who went to SB to the circus and
    while in SB "he bought a suitcase full of

liquor, and when he came back late that afternoon he and WB got drunk." WB later became "ugly-drunk."

5. Fox   BK, MG, MS, PA, PF
   Maude A. Fox, "Willie Boy's Last Stand," *Desert Spotlight,* May–June, 1946, pp. 7, 10.
   Nonfiction. Sources: Reche. Shorter version than that used in her 1954 book (no. 8).

6. Russell   A/D, MG, MS, WL
   Maud Carrico Russell, "The Willie Boy Tragedy," *Desert Spotlight,* June, 1948, pp. 4, 13.
   Nonfiction. Sources: Ben de Crevecoeur, unacknowledged.

7. Spell   A/D, MG, MS
   Hazel M. Spell, *The Twentynine Palms Story* (privately printed, 1953; 3d ed., 1959), pp. 4–5.
   Nonfiction. Sources: Reche; de Crevecoeur without credit.

8. Fox   BK, DS, MG, MS, PA, PF
   Maude A. Fox, *Both Sides of the Mountain* (Palm Desert, Calif.: Desert Magazine Press, 1954), pp. 53–60.
   Nonfiction. Source: Reche.

9. O'Neal   A/D, BK, MG, PA, PF
   Lulu Rasmussen O'Neal, *A Peculiar Piece of the Desert: The Story of California's Morongo Basin* (Los Angeles: Westernlore Press, 1957; reprint [with same pagination], Morongo Valley, Calif.: Sagebrush Press, 1981), pp. 44–47.

Nonfiction. Sources: local lore, usual ones but not acknowledged.

10. Copeland   A/D, IU, MG, ND, PA, PF, WL
John Q. Copeland, "Manhunt at 29 Palms," *Duel,* Summer 1957, pp. 20–21, 71–74.
Nonfiction. Sources: Reche and Toutain "the two possemen surviving today" (p. 71). Exposes tensions between Reche and de Crevecoeur during the chase, and the sheriffs of each county (pp. 71, 72). Reche thought WB a bad Indian; Toutain thought him a good one (p. 72).

139

11. Lawton   A/D, BK, DS, IU, KW, MG, MS, ND, OW, PA, PF, RS, TV
Harry Lawton, *Willie Boy: A Desert Manhunt* (Balboa Island, Calif.: Paisano Press, 1960; 2d ed., Morongo, Calif.: Malki Museum Press, 1976).
So-called nonfiction novel. Sources: Toutain, Reche, de Crevecoeur, and several printed sources, including newspaper coverage of the time and federal records then open. Sees earlier brush with the law for drunkenness.

12. Shumway   A/D, BK, IU, MG, MS, PA, TV, WL
Nina Paul Shumway, *Your Desert and Mine* (Los Angeles: Westernlore Press, 1960), pp. 26–33.
Nonfiction. Sources: Carling and, through him, de Crevecoeur. Also Lawton unacknowledged (TV). (See no. 1.)

13. Edwards   A/D, MG, PF, RS
E. I. Edwards, *Lost Oases along the Carrizo*

(Los Angeles: Westernlore Press, 1961), pp. 94–95. Reviews Lawton's book and gives his own 100-word version of what happened.

Nonfiction (L).

14. Lansford   A/D, DS, IU, MG, PA, RS
W. Douglas Lansford, "Savage Manhunt," *Man's Conquest,* June 1963, pp. 24–27, 42–48.

Nonfiction (L). Sources: not given, but internal evidence indicates Hughes and very obviously Lawton because Lansford even misspells de Crevecoeur the way Lawton does, as "de Crevecouer." Calls WB Billy Boy from the beginning and uses the term *haikoyam* (both on p. 24) for whites from Lawton, p. 38. Erroneously places Ben rather than Wal at the ambush at Ruby Mountain and, following Lawton's error, has the posse mounted. Has Chino playing Hyde's role in running for help (does not even have Hyde in the group).

15. Young   A/D, BK, IU, MG, OW, PA, PF, RS
Bob Young, "They'll Kill You, Willie Boy," *Real West,* July 1966, pp. 26–28, 42–44.

Nonfiction (L). Sources: Claims no. 23, but not then published. Lawton unacknowledged.

16. Evans and Wilson   OW
Caroline Evans and Joan Wilson, eds., *Remembrance of the High Desert* (Yucaipa Valley, Calif.: Artcraft Print Shop, 1966), p. 46.

Nonfiction. Sources: not given.

17. San Bernardino Sheriff's Association
    (henceforth SBDOSA), no. 1   MG, TV
    "They Called Him Willy Boy, the Mad Dog of
    the Morongos," *San Bernardino Sheriff's As-
    sociation Newsletter,* 1966, pp. 114–15.
    Nonfiction (L). Sources: not given, apparently
    Lawton. Nothing about liquor. The 1905 inci-
    dent is called unruliness after WB hit a home
    run in a baseball game in Victorville.

18. SBDOSA, no. 2   MG, TV
    "The Willie Boy Legend Lives On," *San Ber-
    nardino Sheriff's Association Newsletter,* 1967,
    p. 128.
    Nonfiction (L). Sources: Not given but obviously
    Lawton. No liquor mentioned; repeats earlier
    version.

19. Dominguez   MG, MS, ND
    Hansjacob Seiler, "Willie Boy: A Western Dra-
    ma," *Indian Historian* 1 (Winter 1968): 26–
    27.
    Nonfiction. Source: Chona Dominguez, age nine-
    ty-eight, interviewed in July 1955, his main
    Cahuilla "informant" and last surviving mono-
    lingual. She died in 1963. She lived around
    Thermal in the Coachella Valley, and her ac-
    count is based upon hearsay. Her primary
    observation is, "They [the posse] pursued him
    but they never got near him."

20. Evans   A/D, BK, MG, PA, PF, RS
    Rosemary Evans, "Saga of Willie Boy," *Califor-
    nia Traveler,* December 1968, pp. 9–11, 31.

Nonfiction (L). Sources: Malki Museum at Morongo Reservation and Lawton, unacknowledged. See also no. 25.

21. Wilson   MG, MS
    Harry Lawton, *The Last Western Manhunt: Riverside County Sheriff Frank Wilson's Official Report on the Willie Boy Manhunt of 1909* (Ramona, Calif.: Acoma Books, 1970).
    Nonfiction. Sources: hearsay at the time, some observation. No mention of alcohol or Taft visit.

22. Weight   A/D, DS, PA, RS
    Lucile Weight, "The People of the Oasis," *Pioneer Days Souvenir Edition,* October 2, 1975, pp. 6–38.
    Nonfiction. Sources: personal reminiscences of old timers, herself, and census records for 1900, all about Twentynine Palms.

23. True   A/D, IU, KW, MG, PA, WL
    Harry Lawton and Clara True, "The Willie Boy Case and Attendant Circumstances," *Journal of California Anthropology* 5 (Summer 1978): 115–22.
    Nonfiction. Sources: Observation, hearsay especially from Indians and Indian police.

24. Weir   A/D, MG, PA
    T. C. Weir, "The Flight of Willie Boy: A Saga of Desert Survival," *Desert,* August 1980, pp. 42–44.
    Nonfiction (L).

25. Evans   A/D, BK, MG, PA, PF
    Rosemary Evans, "California's Last 'Old West'
    Manhunt," *True West,* March–April, 1981, pp.
    52–53.
    Nonfiction (L). Sources: local press and Malki
    Museum, Lawton unacknowledged.

26. Erickson   A/D, IU, MG, MS
    Rick Erickson, "Willie Boy," *Hi Desert Star,*
    "Grubstake Days," May 20, 1983, pp. 22–29.
    Nonfiction. Sources: local newspapers, True re-
    port, Carling, Wilson but omits Lawton.

27. Bare   MG, MS, TV
    Bill Bare, "Tracking Willie Boy," *Highway Pa-
    trolman,* July 1984, pp. 132–34, 137–38.
    Nonfiction (L). Sources: Lawton, Carling. Ob-
    serves that "each year the story is told, in
    various forms, in local desert newspapers. It's
    as though the chase continues in the deserts
    surrounding Ruby Mountain" (p. 138).

28. Helm   A/D, BK, MG, MS, PA, PF
    Pat Helm, "Willie Boy Story," in *Yucca Valley:
    Reflections of the Past,* vol. 2, comp. Joan
    Wilson (Yucca Valley, Calif., 1985), pp. 12–15.
    Nonfiction (L). Sources: Lawton and Fox. Un-
    dersheriff said that BK was "common among
    the Paiutes" (p. 15).

29. Thrapp   MG
    Dan L. Thrapp, *Encyclopedia of Frontier Biog-
    raphy,* vol. 3 (Glendale, Calif.: Arthur H.
    Clark, 1988), p. 1576.

Nonfiction (L). Sources: Abbreviated Evans (no. 25).

30. Reese   IU, MG
Rex Reese, "Willie Boy: The End of the Trail," *Four Wheeler,* July 1988, pp. 166–67.
Nonfiction (L) and travel. Source: Lawton unacknowledged.

31. Edwards   A/D, IU, MG, MS, PA, TV
Harold L. Edwards, "Willie Boy and the Posses," *The Californians,* November–December, 1989, pp. 48–54.
Nonfiction. Sources: Local newspapers and Wilson. Aims to correct Lawton.

32. Anonymous   A/D, BK, MG, TV
Anonymous, "Willie Boy's Grave," *Hi Desert Star,* "The Desert Trail," April 4, 1991.
Nonfiction (L). Source: Lawton unacknowledged.

33. Hearn   A/D, BK, MG, OW, TV
Stephen T. Hearn, "An Indian Outlaw, a Posse, and a Legend," *Hi Desert Star,* "Sunday Magazine," May 5, 1991.
Nonfiction (L). Source: Lawton unacknowledged.

34. Apodaca   BK, IU
Paul Apodaca, Review of *Willie Boy: A Desert Manhunt, News From Native California,* May–July, 1991, pp. 36–37.
Nonfiction (L). Praises the work as a "classic in Western writing," thirty-one years after its initial publication.

Notes

CHAPTER 1

1. While we are concerned here with the crisis in history, the failure of confidence in intellectual disciplines is more widespread. For a history of higher education in America, the emergence of the crisis, and the current condition of "The Social Nonsciences" and "The Inhuman Humanities," see Smith, *Killing the Spirit,* especially chaps. 15 and 16.

2. For example, see Berkhofer, "Cultural Pluralism versus Ethnocentrism in the New Indian History."

3. Martin, *American Indian and the Problem of History,* "Introduction: An Introduction aboard the Fidèle" and "Epilogue: Time and the American Indian," pp. 3–26, 192–220.

4. Kloppenberg, "Objectivity and Historicism," quoted at p. 1018.

5. Note, for example, the following books, listed alphabetically by author: Axtell, *After Columbus*; Berkhofer, *White Man's Indian*; Hoxie, *Indians versus the Textbooks*; Jennings, *Invasion of America*; Phillips, *Chiefs and Challengers*; and Trigger, *Natives and Newcomers.*

6. The family name of William Mike and the name of his daughter as Carlota are corrections we have added to the story from our interview with William Mike's

grandson, Joe Benitez, on the Cabazon Reservation, February 4, 1989.

7. Lawton, *Willie Boy,* pp. viii–xii.

8. *Los Angeles Herald Examiner,* "California Living," March 29, 1970, p. 7.

9. *Los Angeles Herald Examiner,* "California Living," March 29, 1970, p. 7.

10. Michael Wilmington, "Cowboys and Indians with a Conscience," *Los Angeles Times,* "Calendar," December 16, 1990, p. 39.

11. Melville, *The Confidence Man,* chap. 26, quoted at pp. 179, 180.

12. See the provocative discussion by Drinnon in his *Facing West.*

13. Turner, *Spirit of Place,* pp. 12–15. See also chapter 10 for his provocative discussion of Leslie Marmon Silko's *Ceremony;* Fox, *Pagans and Christians,* pp. 11–23.

14. Pearce, "The Metaphysics of Indian-Hating," p. 30.

15. Davis, *The Return of Martin Guerre,* pp. vii–ix.

16. Laird, *The Chemehuevis,* p. 5.

17. Murray, *Forked Tongues,* pp. 1–126, for the crisis in ethnography, and chapter 7, "Dialogues and Dialogics," for his thoughts on overcoming it.

18. Laird, *The Chemehuevis,* pp. 154–56.

CHAPTER 2

1. James Guthrie to Pierce Lonargan, August 4, 1960, Lawton Papers.

2. *An Illustrated History of Southern California,* p. 478.

3. O'Neal, Appendix, item no. 9, p. 111; Hughes, Appendix, item no. 3, pp. 108–9, 122. (Henceforth, Appendix items are cited simply as A9, A3, etc.)

4. "Report of the Mission Indian Commissioners, December 7, 1891" (hereafter "Smiley Commission Report").

5. "Smiley Commission Report"; Hughes, A3, pp. 148–49.

6. "Smiley Commission Report."

7. *Twenty-sixth Annual Report of the Board of Indian Commissioners, 1894*, p. 15.

8. *Report of the Twenty-sixth Annual Meeting of the Lake Mohonk Conference of Friends of the Indian and Other Dependent Peoples*, p. 25.

9. *Report of the Twenty-sixth Annual Meeting*, pp. 25, 30. On p. 14 Leupp called his women appointees his "Amazonian corps."

10. True, "The Experiences of a Woman Indian Agent," p. 331.

11. Section 16, Supervisor Harwood Hall, General Inspection of Malki, California, June 1, 1909, Office of Indian Affairs File no. 43933–09. During her tenure as Indian agent, Clara True renamed Morongo as Malki, the name preferred by Indians.

12. Russell, "Old Trails to Twentynine Palms," pp. 2–3.

13. Section 5, Supervisor Charles Davis, General Inspection of Malki, California, March 18, 1910, Office of Indian Affairs File no. 24496–10.

14. Interview with Joe Benitez, grandson of William Mike, February 4, 1989.

15. Interview with Joe Benitez, February 4, 1989.

16. *Redlands Daily Review*, October 5, 1909. The *Banning Record* called him a "Chimewawa" (Chemehuevi) on September 30, 1909, but gave his name as either Willie Boy or Billie Boy (the latter name was wrong). The *Los Angeles Herald* also began with the

Billy Boy name on September 27, 1909, but quickly
dropped it.

17. *Riverside Morning Mission,* October 9, 1909.

18. Fox, A5, pp. 7, 10.

19. *World 1909 Almanac and Encyclopedia,* pp. 50–
51. See also *Redlands Daily Review* and *Banning Record,* October 9, 1909.

20. *Riverside Morning Mission,* October 7, 1909.

21. *Redlands Citrograph,* March 4, 1905; September 8, 1906.

22. *Los Angeles Daily Times,* October 12, 1909; *Redlands Daily Review,* October 17, 1909.

23. Harwood Hall to Clara True, June 13, 1908, Records of the Superintendent, Sherman Institute.

24. *Report of the Twenty-sixth Annual Meeting,* p. 29 (True's emphasis).

25. *San Bernardino Daily Sun,* October 14, 1909; *Riverside Morning Mission,* October 16, 1909; *Los Angeles Daily Times,* October 11, 14–16, 1909; *Los Angeles Record,* October 15, 1909.

26. Christina Wagner, widow of Randolph Madison, to Harry Lawton, April 20, 1958, Lawton Papers. See also Madison's story in the *Seattle Star,* October 13, 1909.

27. Madison story in the *Seattle Star,* October 16, 1909.

28. The most detailed report is in the *Los Angeles Herald,* October 16, 1909.

29. Mat of Madison's story of October 16, 1909, datelined San Francisco (Newspaper Enterprise Association Archive).

CHAPTER 3

1. Hughes, A3, p. 173.

2. Harry Lawton to Horace Parker, mid-April 1957, Parker Papers.

3. Paul, A1, pp. 24–26, 56–64, quoted at p. 58.

4. Shumway, A12, pp. 26–33.

5. Wood, A2, p. 10.

6. Wood, A2, p. 13.

7. Hughes, A3, p. 173.

8. Carling, A4, pp. 6–11, quoted at p. 6. At the time of the chase, Randolph Madison filed a story reading, "Near the spot where they found the body of little Mary Nita or Isoleta as she was known among her people, were strange hieroglyphics marked on a limestone formation with a piece of harder stone. Segundo Chino and Jack Hyde, two of our trailers [trackers], interpreted them as follows: 'My heart is gone. I soon will be dead.' It was thought that the heart broken and wearied girl traced this final message the night before she was killed by her ruthless abductor" (*Seattle Star,* October 16, 1909).

9. Shipley, "Native Languages of California," pp. 80–90. The education of the young woman will be discussed in chapter 5.

10. Horace Parker to Harry Lawton, April 20, 1957, Lawton Papers.

11. Harry Lawton to Horace Parker, mid-April, 1957, Parker Papers.

12. Ben de Crevecoeur claimed to have heard the girl weeping during the initial pursuit, the period when the posse was supposedly close enough to hear but not capture the fugitives, and he described Reche's finding her corpse and describing the condition of the body. But in neither of these instances was he present.

13. Fox, A5, all, and A8, pp. 53–58; Russell, A6, pp. 10, 13; Spell, A7, pp. 4–5.

14. Copeland, A10, pp. 20–21, 71–74.

15. *Redlands Daily Facts,* October 12, 1909.

16. Cited in the *Banning Record,* December 30, 1909.

17. *Banning Record,* March 31, 1910.

18. Lawton, *Willie Boy,* p. viii.

19. Bataille and Silet, "The Entertaining Anachronism," p. 38.

20. Lawton, *Willie Boy,* p. x and unpaginated beginning. The epigraph is from Egan, *Pioneering the West, 1846–1878,* pp. 252–53.

21. Harry Lawton to Horace Parker, [November?] 1959, Parker Papers.

22. Lawton, *Willie Boy,* pp. 7, 64–65.

23. Lawton may have been following the practice of Randolph Madison, whose stories datelined from San Francisco on October 12 and 19, 1909, bear an editor's note "Mat of Billy Boy was sent you in the San Francisco sheet of October 12" (Newspaper Enterprise Association Archive).

24. Lawton, *Willie Boy,* beginning on p. 1.

25. The description is Nabokov's in *Lolita: A Screenplay,* p. x.

26. At one point Lawton had another idea for her name. "I prefer Isoleta, but it sounds like someone has been reading *Tristan and Isolt*" (Harry Lawton to Horace Parker, mid-April 1957, Parker Papers).

27. Lawton, *Willie Boy,* pp. 1–6.

28. Harry Lawton to Horace Parker, January 30 and February 7, 1958, Parker Papers.

29. Horace Parker to Harry Lawton, February 4, 1958, Lawton Papers.

30. Lawton, *Willie Boy,* p. xi.

31. We discuss this allegation in detail in chapter 5.

32. Lawton, *Willie Boy,* p. 64.

33. Lawton, *Willie Boy,* pp. 51–52, 60–61. Lawton used the coroner's reports selectively, accepting the

verdict in the death of William Mike but then rejecting it in the death of his daughter.

34. Horace Parker to Harry Lawton, January 31, 1955, Parker Papers.

35. Harry Lawton to Horace Parker, March 18, 1958, Parker Papers.

36. Lawton, *Willie Boy,* pp. 79–83, 108–12.

37. De Crevecoeur family members complain that Lawton misspelled the family name as de Crevecouer throughout his book.

38. Harry Lawton to Horace Parker, mid-April 1957, Parker Papers.

39. Harry Lawton to Horace Parker, December 8, 1958, Parker Papers.

40. Harry Lawton to Horace Parker, June 24, 1959, Parker Papers.

41. Their words of praise are printed on the back cover of the second edition.

42. Larry Burgess interview with Frank Moore; *Redlands Daily Facts,* May 11 and 16, 1961.

43. Larry Burgess interview with Judy Parker Hancock, daughter of Horace Parker.

44. Lawton, *Willie Boy,* p. 194.

45. Jane Penn to Harry Lawton, March 7, 1960, Lawton Papers (word order rearranged slightly).

46. Evans, A20, p. 9.

47. Lawton was chairman of the Malki Museum publications program when his novel was reprinted. See Jennings, "Morongo's Malki Museum," p. 37.

48. SBDOSA, no. 1, A17, p. 116.

49. Wilson, A21.

50. Apodaca, A34.

51. Bare, A27, p. 138; SBDOSA, no. 1, A17, p. 116.

52. Lansford, A14, pp. 24–27, 42–48.

53. Edwards, A31, pp. 48–54, Barnes's poem is an inset on p. 53. Barnes had originally sent a copy of the poem to Lawton in July 1984 (Lawton Papers).

54. Anonymous, A32. In 1992 a local reporter wrote that "the entire event is in honor of the lawmen of the west who risked their lives tracking the renegade." She also reported that "all kinds of horses are ridden to the site where Willie Boy, an outlaw, was shot by members of the last known organized posse." See Susan Chaney, "Willie Boy Days 'a Success,'" *Hi Desert Star*, May 10, 1992.

55. Dave Miller, "Willie Boy Days Expands to Community Fair," and advertising supplement, *Hi-Desert Star*, "Sunday Magazine and Basin Life," May 5, 1991.

CHAPTER 4

1. Rice, "And Afterwards, Take Him to a Movie," pp. 43–44, 71.

2. Bataille and Silet, "The Entertaining Anachronism," pp. 43–44; Georgakas, "They Have Not Spoken," pp. 26–32.

3. For thoughtful Native American reaction to *Dances with Wolves*, see Seals, "The New Custerism," pp. 634–39; Elliott, "America Loves Indians," p. 25A; Castillo, "Review, *Dances with Wolves*," pp. 14–23.

4. See, for example, Friar and Friar, *The Only Good Indian;* Bataille and Silet, "The Indian in American Film," pp. 171–82; O'Connor, *The Hollywood Indian;* Oshana, "Native American Women in Westerns," pp. 46–50; Bataille and Silet, "Economic and Psychic Exploitation of American Indians," pp. 8–21.

5. Tuska, *The American West in Film*, pp. 17, 35–36.

6. Tuska, *The American West In Film*, p. 17.

7. *Willie Boy,* Early Draft; First Draft Screenplay no. 00889; Final Screenplay no. 02023; all in Lawton Papers.

8. Polonsky's use of the Ghost Dance symbolism was intentional; he also wanted to use an epigraph from a Ghost Dancer's song, "My father, have pity on me. . . . everything is gone!" to introduce the film. Instead he had a voice-over of a text projected onto the screen telling the audience that the story about to unfold really happened. See also Polonsky's interview in Sherman and Rubin, *The Director's Event*, pp. 30–31.

9. Tuska, *The American West in Film*, p. 224.

10. Tuska, *The American West in Film*, pp. 239–41; Friar and Friar, *The Only Good Indian*, pp. 229–45.

11. Sherman and Rubin, *The Director's Event*, p. 36.

12. Of course, one could purchase liquor *illegally* in Riverside County then. In 1909, however, Clara True had made it impossible for bootleggers to sell on the reservation. And the builder and host of the Mission Inn, Frank Miller, personally opposed alcohol and never sold it in his establishment as long as he owned it.

13. Perhaps Blake was reading from the wrong script. Polonsky gave the incorrect number in his Early Draft of *Willie Boy* but corrected it in the First Draft Screenplay and Final Screenplay. Somehow the wrong number got into the film.

14. Harry Hunt to Harry Lawton, February 11, 1958, Lawton Papers.

15. True, "The Experiences of a Woman Indian Agent," p. 333.

16. Carl Nelson to Harry Lawton, March 1, 1960, Lawton Papers.

17. Sherman and Rubin, *The Director's Event,* p. 25.

18. Kael, "Americana," pp. 47–50.

19. Friar and Friar, *The Only Good Indian,* pp. 255, 266.

20. Tuska, *The American West in Film,* p. 147 (Tuska's emphasis). The context was a discussion of film biographies of Jesse James.

21. A scene that persisted through all three screenplays, although much abbreviated in the final, never made the final cut, if it was filmed at all. It depicted a town Chemehuevi dressed in his "Sunday best" looking at a group of desert Chemehuevi and denigrating them to the Paiute Willie Boy as "grasshopper eaters" and rude folk who made Indians like himself and Willie Boy look "lousy." The very existence of the scene and the use of the slur indicate that Polonsky was beginning to learn intertribal rivalries and animosities.

CHAPTER 5

1. Larry Burgess interview with Edgar Fisher. Fisher had lived in the community since 1907, having arrived as a twenty-one-year-old immigrant from England.

2. Clara True to the Commissioner of Indian Affairs, October 20, 1909, "The Willie Boy Case and Attendant Circumstances," Section 13, "Willie Boy," in the Report of Harwood Hall, General Inspection Malki School, California, October 22, 1909, Office of Indian Affairs file no. 79987-09 (hereafter Clara True's document will be cited as True Report, and Harwood Hall's as Hall Inspection). Lawton published the True Report in 1978. See True, A23.

3. Undated Harry Lawton interview with Jim McInnis of Hesperia, Lawton Papers.

4. Undated Harry Lawton interview with James "Dad" Goulding and Miss Goulding, Lucerne Valley, Lawton Papers.

5. Copeland, A10, p. 72.

6. Harry Lawton to Horace Parker, mid-April 1957, Parker Papers.

7. Copeland, A10, p. 72. The quotation is Copeland's description of Toutain's thoughts.

8. Hughes, A3, p. 122.

9. Lawton, *Willie Boy*, p. xi.

10. Notes (p. 1, n. 2; p. 4, n. 17) to unpublished version of *Willie Boy*, Lawton Papers.

11. There was a "Robles" associated with the incident in a minor way, one Teofilo or Tefflie Robles of San Bernardino. Robles, an Indian, had been arrested in San Bernardino when he tried to join the posse in pursuit of Willie Boy. He had purchased a handgun with money he had stolen from two young Indian males (*San Bernardino Daily Sun*, October 9, 1909). In *Willie Boy*, pp. 121–23, Lawton presents an account of Robles's arrest and subsequent prison term that differs significantly from the newspaper version.

12. Harry Lawton to Horace Parker, April 3, 1958, Parker Papers.

13. Dorris, *The Broken Cord*, p. 84. Dorris poignantly describes his life with his adopted son Adam, who, as Dorris discovered several years after adoption, suffered from fetal alcohol syndrome. This account and the bibliography included constitute an important departure point for inquiry into the effect of alcohol upon Native Americans.

14. Otto Sweeters (born in Banning in 1889, died in Yucaipa in 1963) was the fourth of six children born to German immigrant parents. Otto's father ran Banning's

sole saloon until the county voted dry in 1893. The elder Sweeters then went into ranching. Otto's older brother, Clem A. Sweeters, engaged in many public activities, including law enforcement; he was elected Riverside County sheriff in 1926. Otto Sweeters worked as an electrician. See Hughes, A3, pp. 42–43, 54, 57, 147–48; obituary of Otto Sweeters, *Redlands Daily Facts,* October 17, 1963; tombstone of Otto Sweeters, Mountain View Cemetery, Beaumont, California.

15. *New York Sun* and *New York World,* October 13, 1909.

16. *N. W. Ayer and Son's American Newspaper Annual and Directory, 1909,* pp. 611, 614 for New York; pp. 67–70 for Redlands, Riverside, and San Bernardino; pp. 43–44 for Los Angeles.

17. *Riverside Morning Mission,* October 15, 1909.

18. *Riverside Morning Mission,* October 15, 1909.

19. See Appendix items 11, 12, 17, 18, 27, 31, 32, 33.

20. For example, Fox, A8, p. 56.

21. True Report.

22. Remarks made by Donald S. C. Anderson at the Fortnightly Club gathering, Redlands, California, January 3, 1991.

23. For example, *Riverside Morning Mission,* October 16, 1909.

24. True Report and surrounding documents.

25. "Reports of the Departments of the Colorado and of California," *United States War Department Annual Reports, 1910,* vol. 3, pp. 119–51.

26. Wilson, A21.

27. Lawton, *Willie Boy,* p. viii.

28. Burr Belden to Harry Lawton, February 22 [1960], Lawton Papers. For the articles, see the Belden Papers.

CHAPTER 6

1. Sister Eileen Cotter, professor emerita of English from the University of Redlands who works among the Indians at the Morongo Reservation, introduced us to Joe.

2. Gayle Benitez to Harry Lawton, October 15, 1966, Lawton Papers. For the information he gleaned from Dot Benitez, see Harry Lawton to Horace Parker, two letters undated and labeled mid-April 1957 and September 9, 1959, Parker Papers.

3. Hall Inspection.

4. True Report.

5. Laird, *The Chemehuevis*, pp. xxiv–xxvii.

6. Awonawilona Harrington, "The Chemehuevi: Their Name, Character, and Habitat," in *Chemehuevi*, Harrington Papers, vol. 3, reel 147, frames 0460–0471.

7. Kroeber, *Handbook of the Indians of California*. The original letter of transmittal recommending publication was dated February 18, 1919.

8. D'Azevedo, *Great Basin*, pp. 277, 292, 624.

9. Laird, *The Chemehuevis*, pp. 21–22.

10. Bailey, *Weather of Southern California*, pp. 11–15.

11. Bailey, *Weather of Southern California*, pp. 40–42.

12. Laird, *The Chemehuevis*, pp. 9–21.

13. Laird, *The Chemehuevis*, pp. 47–48. The Indian's name, in English, was Rat Penis. At one point George Laird described the runners as his cousins (p. 249 n. 1).

14. P. Nabokov, *Indian Running*, p. 70.

15. See, for example, Lawton, *Willie Boy*, p. 52; Fox, A8, p. 58.

16. Laird, *The Chemehuevis*, p. 70.

17.   Thornton, *American Indian Holocaust and Survival*, p. 136 n. 2.

18.   Mooney, *The Ghost-Dance Religion and Wounded Knee*, pp. 764–77, quoted at p. 764. See also Moses, " 'The Father Tells Me So!' Wovoka," pp. 335–51.

19.   Hittman, *Wovoka and the Ghost Dance*, pp. 57, 79, 278, the most complete study of the subject, presents evidence that while sobriety was an essential element of the Ghost Dance message, the Prophet did not personally preach it or any other remedial behavior to his followers.

20.   Moses, " 'The Father Tells Me So!' Wovoka."

21.   Laird, *The Chemehuevis*, p. 44.

22.   Laird, *The Chemehuevis*, pp. 15, 73–77, 242 n. 18.

23.   Laird, *The Chemehuevis*, p. 49.

24.   Laird, *The Chemehuevis*, pp. 45, 70–81. One of the runners specifically named as affected by the Ghost Dance was Rat Penis, although he apparently did not leave the river. A boy about ten years younger than Rat Penis and his constant companion was called Fish Vagina. While these names may imply a homosexual relationship, Carobeth Laird did not pursue the subject of same-sex relationships in Chemehuevi culture, even though the subject is mentioned in the myth "How Horned Toad Visited the Giants," pp. 160–61. Williams, *The Spirit and the Flesh*, pp. 11–14, points out that many anthropologists have been reluctant to discuss same-sex relations with Indians. Williams goes on to note that the Mojave, neighbors to the Chemehuevi, have an open attitude toward same-sex relations between men and boys (pp. 89–90).

25.   Moses, " 'The Father Tells Me So!' Wovoka," p. 336.

26. Twelfth Census of the United States, 1900, Individual Census Schedules, California, T-623, R 97. Willie Boy's sister was Georgia Bruce.

27. Laird, *The Chemehuevis*, pp. 152–54.

28. For example, *Riverside Morning Mission*, October 7, 1909.

29. SBDOSA, no. 1, A17.

30. Mooney, *The Ghost-Dance Religion and Wounded Knee*, pp. 772, 775.

31. This relationship may not have been as precise as English suggests. "The [Chemehuevi] myths have shown us that siblings, especially siblings of the same sex, tend to be regarded as replicas of each other, mere divisions of a single entity. Perhaps this accounts for the use of the same terms for 'siblings' and 'cousins.' . . . This would account for the feeling that sexual relationships between cousins were just as incestuous-as between brother and sister" (Laird, *The Chemehuevis*, p. 55). The point is that Willie Boy and Carlota violated tribal taboo, regardless of the degree of family tie.

32. True Report.

33. Interview with Joe Benitez, February 4, 1989.

34. Laird, *The Chemehuevis*, pp. xxv–xxvi. In our interview with Mary Lou Brown, however, Carobeth Laird was described as a homewrecker.

35. Interview with Joe Benitez, February 4, 1989.

36. Harry Lawton to Doc Parker, September 9, 1959, Parker Papers, relating conversation with Dot Rogers.

37. Carobeth Laird, "Behavioral Patterns in Chemehuevi Myths," pp. 97–103, quoted at p. 100.

38. True Report.

39. Interview with Joe Benitez, August 12, 1989.

40. Russell, "Early Days of Twentynine Palms," pp. 6, 11, 14.

41. Interview with Joe Benitez, August 12, 1989.

CHAPTER 8

1. Edwards, A13.

2. Interview with Adrian Fisher, January 5, 1991. We are drawing on all our conversations with Chemehuevis for this reconstruction but will cite only specific discussions for a particular detail.

3. True Report.

4. Coroner Records, 1909, p. 146.

5. True Report.

6. Notes (p. 5, n. 15) to unpublished ms version of *Willie Boy,* Lawton Papers; interview with Joe Benitez, February 4, 1989.

7. Census, Morongo Reservation, June 30, 1906.

8. Interviews with Alberta Van Fleet, January 5 and February 15, 1991.

9. Notes (p. 5, n. 24) to unpublished ms version of *Willie Boy,* Lawton Papers.

10. Interview with Joe Benitez, February 4, 1989.

11. True Report. Clara True could communicate with the Chemehuevis only in Spanish or English. See Russell, "Old Trails to Twentynine Palms," p. 3.

12. *Riverside Morning Mission,* October 2, 1909.

13. Bailey, *Weather of Southern California,* pp. 40–42.

14. Coroner Records, 1909, p. 147.

15. As previously noted in the text, Lawton dismissed the coroner's report, a surprising act, given the supposition of his publisher, Horace Doc Parker, that a member of the posse had accidently killed the young woman (see Doc to Harry Lawton, April 7, 1961, Law-

ton Collection). We did not discover the Lawton Papers until after we had drawn our own conclusions about Carlota's death.

16. Interviews with Alberta Van Fleet and Mary Lou Brown.

17. True Report.

18. Gayton, "The Ghost Dance of 1870 in South-Central California," pp. 57–82, esp pp. 78–79.

19. Christina Wagner, widow of Randolph Madison, to Harry Lawton, April 20 and June 11, 1958; September 30, 1959, Lawton Papers.

20. Awonawilona Harrington, "The Chemehuevi."

21. Laird, *The Chemehuevis,* p. 53. As will be recalled from chapter 6, that taboo no longer obtains.

22. Interview with Joe Benitez, March 23, 1991.

CHAPTER 9

1. Limerick, *The Legacy of Conquest,* p. 349.

2. Bean, "Memorial to Jane K. Penn (1910–1980)," pp. 3–5.

3. Pearce, "The Metaphysics of Indian-Hating," p. 35.

4. See the "AHR Forum" in *American Historical Review* 93 (December 1988): 1173–1227; and again in 97 (April 1992): 487–511.

5. Drinnon, *Facing West.*

6. Wolf, *Europe and the People without History.* See also Sheridan, "How to Tell the Story of a 'People without History,'" pp. 168–89.

Bibliography

UNPUBLISHED SOURCES
Personal Papers
Belden, L. Burr. A. K. Smiley Public Library, Redlands, California.
Harrington, John Peabody. National Anthropological Archives, Smithsonian Institution, Washington, D.C.
Lawton, Harry. Special Collections, Rivera Library, University of California, Riverside.
Parker, Horace "Doc." Sherman Library, Corona del Mar, California.

Other Manuscript Collections
Census. Morongo Reservation, June 30, 1906. Indian Census Rolls, 1895–1940. Department of the Interior. National Archives Microfilm Publications, Microcopy 595.
Coroner Records, 1909. Riverside County, California.
Newspaper Enterprise Association Archive. United Media, New York.
Office of Indian Affairs. Bureau of Indian Affairs. Records of the Inspection Division: 1908–1940, Malki, Department of the Interior. Record Group 75. National Archives.
"Report of the Mission Indian Commissioners, December 7, 1891." Department of the Interior. Copy in

A. K. Smiley Papers, A. K. Smiley Public Library, Redlands, California.

Sherman Institute Records. Bureau of Indian Affairs. Department of the Interior. Record Group 75. National Archives. Laguna Niguel Federal Records Center.

Twelfth Census of the United States, 1900. Office of the Census. Record Group 29. National Archives.

163

Interviews (with both authors, unless noted otherwise)
Chemehuevis
Benitez, Joe. Cabazon Reservation, California, February 4 and August 12, 1989; February 10, 1990; March 23, 1991

Brown, Mary Lou. Colorado River Indian Tribes (CRIT) Reservation, Parker, Arizona, February 15, 1991.

Fisher, Adrian. CRIT Reservation, January 5 and February 15, 1991.

Lytle, Patrick. CRIT Reservation, February 15, 1991.

Van Fleet, Alberta. CRIT Reservation, January 5 and February 15, 1991.

Others
Cotter, Eileen. Banning, California, October 4, 1988.

Fisher, Edgar. Interview with Larry E. Burgess, Redlands, California, April 12, 1990.

Hancock, Judy Parker. Interview with Larry E. Burgess, Kamuela, Hawaii, March 23, 1990.

Moore, Frank. Interview with Larry E. Burgess, Redlands, California, November 28, 1990.

PUBLISHED SOURCES
Books
Axtell, James. *After Columbus: Essays in the Ethnohistory of Colonial North America*. New York: Oxford University Press, 1988.

Bailey, Harry P. *Weather of Southern California*. Berkeley: University of California Press, 1966.

Berkhofer, Robert, Jr. *The White Man's Indian: Images of the American Indian from Columbus to the Present*. New York: Alfred A. Knopf, 1976.

Davis, Natalie Zemon. *The Return of Martin Guerre*. Cambridge: Harvard University Press, 1983.

D'Azevedo, Warren L., ed. *Great Basin*. Vol. 11 of *Handbook of North American Indians*. Washington, D.C.: Smithsonian Institution, 1986.

Dorris, Michael. *The Broken Cord*. New York: Harper and Row, 1989.

Drinnon, Richard. *Facing West: The Metaphysics of Indian Hating and Empire Building*. Minneapolis: University of Minnesota Press, 1980.

Egan, William M., ed. and comp. *Pioneering the West, 1846–1878: Major Howard Egan's Diary*. Richmond, Utah: Howard R. Egan Estate, 1917.

Fox, Robin Lane. *Pagans and Christians*. New York: Alfred A. Knopf, 1989.

Friar, Ralph E., and Natasha A. Friar. *The Only Good Indian . . . The Hollywood Gospel*. New York: Drama Book Specialists/Publishers, 1972.

Hittman, Michael. *Wovoka and the Ghost Dance*. Yerington, Nev.: Yerington Paiute Tribe, through a grant from the Grace Dangberg Foundation, 1990.

Hoxie, Frederick E. *The Indians versus the Textbooks: Is There Any Way Out?* Chicago: D'Arcy McNickle Center for the Study of the American Indian, Newberry Library, 1984.

An Illustrated History of Southern California, Chicago: Lewis Publishing, 1890.

Jennings, Francis. *The Invasion of America: Indians, Colonialism, and the Cant of Conquest*. Chapel Hill:

University of North Carolina Press, 1975.

Kroeber, Alfred L. *Handbook of the Indians of California*. 1925. Reprint. New York: Dover Publications, 1976.

Laird, Carobeth. *The Chemehuevis*. Banning, Calif.: Malki Museum Press, 1976.

Lawton, Harry. *Willie Boy: A Desert Manhunt*. Balboa Island, Calif.: Paisano Press, 1960.

Limerick, Patricia Nelson. *The Legacy of Conquest: The Unbroken Past of the American West*. New York: W. W. Norton, 1987.

Martin, Calvin, ed. *The American Indian and the Problem of History*. New York: Oxford University Press, 1987.

Melville, Herman. *The Confidence Man: His Masquerade*. New York: Grove Press, 1949.

Miller, Randall M. *The Kaleidoscopic Lens: How Hollywood Views Ethnic Groups*. N.p. Jerome S. Ozer, 1980.

Miller, Ronald Dean, and Peggy Jeanne Miller. *The Chemehuevi Indians of Southern California*. Banning, Calif.: Malki Museum Press, 1967.

Mooney, James. *The Ghost-Dance Religion and Wounded Knee*. 1891. Reprint. New York: Dover Publications, 1973.

Murray, David. *Forked Tongues: Speech, Writing and Representation in North American Indian Texts*. Bloomington: University of Indiana Press, 1991.

N. W. Ayer and Son's *American Newspaper Annual and Directory, 1909*. Philadelphia: N. W. Ayer and Son, 1909.

Nabokov, Peter. *Indian Running: Native American History and Tradition*. Santa Fe: Ancient City Press, 1981.

Nabokov, Vladimir. *Lolita: A Screenplay.* New York: McGraw-Hill, 1974.

Novick, Peter. *That Noble Dream: The "Objectivity Question" and the American Historical Profession.* New York: Cambridge University Press, 1988.

O'Connor, John E. *The Hollywood Indian: Stereotypes of Native Americans in Films.* Trenton, N.J.: New Jersey State Museum, 1980.

Phillips, George Harwood. *Chiefs and Challengers: Indian Resistance and Cooperation in Southern California.* Berkeley: University of California Press, 1975.

Report of the Twenty-sixth Annual Meeting of the Lake Mohonk Conference of Friends of the Indian and Other Dependent Peoples. Lake Mohonk, N.Y.: Lake Mohonk Conference of Friends of the Indian and Other Dependent Peoples, 1908.

Sherman, Eric, and Martin Rubin. *The Director's Event: Interviews with Five American Film-Makers.* New York: Atheneum, 1970.

Smith, Page. *Killing the Spirit: Higher Education in America.* New York: Viking, 1990.

Thornton, Russell. *American Indian Holocaust and Survival: A Population History since 1492.* Norman: University of Oklahoma Press, 1987.

Trigger, Bruce G. *Natives and Newcomers: Canada's "Heroic Age" Reconsidered.* Kingston: McGill-Queen's University Press, 1985.

Turner, Frederick. *Spirit of Place: The Making of an American Literary Landscape.* San Francisco: Sierra Club Books, 1989.

Tuska, Jon. *The American West in Film: Critical Approaches to the Western.* Lincoln: University of Nebraska Press, 1988.

Twenty-sixth Annual Report of the Board of Indian Commissioners, 1894. Washington, D.C.: Government Printing Office, 1895.

United States War Department Annual Report, 1910. 4 vols. Washington, D.C.: Government Printing Office, 1911.

Williams, Walter L. *The Spirit and the Flesh: Sexual Diversity in American Indian Culture.* Boston: Beacon Press, 1986.

Wolf, Eric. *Europe and the People without History.* Berkeley: University of California Press, 1982.

World 1909 Almanac and Encyclopedia. New York: Press Publication, 1909.

167

Articles

Bataille, Gretchen M., and Charles L. P. Silet. "Economic and Psychic Exploitation of American Indians." *Explorations in Ethnic Studies* 6 (July 1983): 8–21.

———. "The Entertaining Anachronism: Indians in American Film." In *The Kaleidoscopic Lens: How Hollywood Views Ethnic Groups,* ed. Randall Miller, pp. 36–53. N.p.: Jerome S. Ozer, 1980.

———. "The Indian in American Film: A Checklist of Published Materials on Popular Images of the Indian in the American Film." *Journal of Popular Film* 5, no. 2 (1976): 171–82.

Bean, Lowell John. "Memorial to Jane K. Penn (1910–1980)." *Journal of California and Great Basin Anthropology* 2 (Summer 1980): 3–5.

Berkhofer, Robert, Jr. "Cultural Pluralism versus Ethnocentrism in the New Indian History." In *The American Indian and the Problem of History,* ed. Calvin Martin, pp. 35–45. New York: Oxford University Press, 1987.

Castillo, Edward D. "Review, *Dances With Wolves.*" *Film Quarterly* 44 (Summer 1991): 14–23.

Elliott, Jan. "America Loves Indians . . . and All That." *Indigenous Thought* 1 (March–June 1991): 25A.

Fehrenbacher, Don E. Written exchange with Gore Vidal over Vidal's *Lincoln. American Historical Review* 96 (February, 1991): 324–28.

Gayton, A. H. "The Ghost Dance of 1870 in South-Central California." *University of California Publications in American Archaeology and Ethnology* 28 (1930–31): 57–82.

Georgakas, Dan. "They Have Not Spoken: American Indians in Film." *Film Quarterly* 25 (Spring 1972): 26–32.

Jennings, Anne. "Morongo's Malki Museum." *Desert* 39 (March 1976): 36–38.

Kael, Pauline. "Americana: *Tell Them Willie Boy Is Here.*" *New Yorker* 45 (December 27, 1969): 47–50.

Kloppenberg, James T. "Objectivity and Historicism: A Century of American Historical Writing. *American Historical Review* 94 (October 1989): 1011–30.

Kroeber, Alfred L. "Ethnography of the Cahuilla Indians." *University of California Publications in American Archaeology and Ethnology* 8 (1908): 29–68.

Laird, Carobeth. "Behavioral Patterns in Chemehuevi Myths." In *Flowers of the Wind: Papers on Ritual, Myth, and Symbolism in California and the Southwest,* ed. Thomas C. Blackburn, pp. 97–103. Socorro, N. Mex.: Ballena Press, 1977.

Limerick, Patricia Nelson. "What on Earth Is the New Western History?" *Montana* 83 (Summer 1990): 61–64.

Moses, L. G. " 'The Father Tells Me So!' Wovoka: The Ghost Dance Prophet." *American Indian Quarterly* 9 (Summer 1985): 335–51.

Oshana, Maryann. "Native American Women in Westerns: Reality and Myth." *Frontiers* 6, no. 3 (1982): 46–50.

Pearce, Roy Harvey. "The Metaphysics of Indian-Hating." *Ethnohistory* 4 (1957): 27–40.

Rice, Susan. "And Afterwards, Take Him to a Movie." *Media and Methods* 7 (April 1971): 43–44, 71.

Russell, Maude Carrico. "Early Days of Twentynine Palms." *Desert Spotlight,* February 1948, pp. 6, 11, 14.

————. "Old Trails to Twentynine Palms." *Desert Spotlight,* December 1946, pp. 2–3.

Seals, David. "The New Custerism." *Nation,* May 13, 1991, pp. 634–39.

Sheridan, Thomas E. "How to Tell the Story of a 'People without History': Narrative versus Ethnohistorical Approaches to the Study of the Yaqui Indians through Time." *Journal of the Southwest* 30 (Summer 1988): 168–89.

Shipley, William. "Native Languages of California." In *California,* ed. Robert Heizer, vol. 8 of *Handbook of North American Indians.* Washington, D.C.: Smithsonian Institution, 1978.

True, Clara. "The Experiences of a Woman Indian Agent." *Outlook* 92 (June 5, 1909): 331–36.

Newspapers
California
Banning Record
The Citrograph
Hi-Desert Star
Los Angeles Daily Times
Los Angeles Herald
Los Angeles Herald Exmainer

Los Angeles Record
Redlands Daily Facts
Redlands Daily Review
Riverside Morning Mission
San Bernardino Sun

Other
New York Sun
New York Times
New York World
Seattle Star

Index

Ainsworth, Ed, 47
Alcohol. *See* Beer; Bootleggers; Champagne; Whiskey
America, as European resource, 12
American Indians: hatred of (*see* Indian-hating); history and, 5–6, 7; worldview of, 5, 10. *See also* Cahuilla Indians; Chemehuevis; Mojave Indians; Morongo Reservation; Paiutes; Sioux
Anderson, Donald S. C., 83
Animals, in Chemehuevi song, 94
"Arnold, Elizabeth." *See* "Liz"

Banning, Calif., 20, 23, 26, 28; Indian-hating in, 74, 129; Indians of (*see* Morongo Reservation)
Banning (Calif.) *Record*, 19, 147n.16
Barnes, Dick, 52, 152n.53
Baseball, Willie Boy and, 102
Beer, as *Tell Them* prop, 65
Belden, Burr, 84
Benitez, Joe, 87, 88, 96, 110, 146n.6
Berkhofer, Robert, 5
Bigotry, Indians and, 13. *See also* Indian-hating
Billy Boy. *See* Willie Boy
Blake, Robert, 9, 57, 153n.13
Boniface, Mike. *See* Mike, William

Bootleggers: Clara True vs., 22, 30–31, 66, 75, 153n.12; on Morongo Reservation, 57, 59
Brown, Mary Lou, 106, 107, 112, 159n.34
Bruce, Georgia, 101, 106, 159n.26
Butch Cassidy and the Sundance Kid (film), 70

Cahuilla Indians: Lawton and, 48–51; in *Tell Them Willie Boy Is Here*, 131
Carling, James, 39
Cereal, as Banning-area crop, 23
Champagne, as *Tell Them* prop, 65
Chemehuevi(s), 15–16, 133–34; as Banning-area migrant labor, 23; and homosexuality, 158n.24; and Paiutes, 90–91; persona of, 90, 97; songs of, 93–94, 97, 99–100, 134 (*see also* Ghost Dance); spiritual world of, 15 (*see also* Ghost Dance; Myths, Chemehuevi); of Twentynine Palms, 92–94, 96–97, 99–102, 105–10, 115, 121–23, 127; white fear of, 32, 84; Willie Boy tragedy in terms of, 113. *See also* Benitez, Joe; Chino, Segundo; Mike, Carlota; Mike, William; Rat Penis; Willie Boy
Cheney, Cliff, 78
Chicago Tribune, 85
Chino, Segundo, 24, 25, 27, 28, 32, 33, 35, 41, 118, 119, 149n.8; and Maria Mike, 106
Christ, Willie Boy as, 69
Christianity, vs. spirituality, 12
Civilization, Polonsky "vs.," 69
Clark, Susan, 57. *See also* "Liz"
Coburn, P. M., 42
Columbus, Christopher, 7, 17, 135
Connell, John, 47
Convict, Willie Boy as, 29, 66, 102
"Coop," 57, 59–66, 68–70, 82
Copeland, John Q., 40, 74, 155n.7

Costner, Kevin, 55, 96
Cotter, Eileen, 157n.1
Crevecoeur. *See* de Crevecoeur
Crosby, Alfred, 7
Custer, George Armstrong, 83

Dances With Wolves (film), 55, 96
Davis, Natalie Zemon, 14
Dead, Chemehuevi dread of, 127, 161n.21
De Crevecoeur, Ben, 20, 24, 30–33, 75–79, 91, 102,
    115, 129–31; death of, 74; as writer source, 37–39, 41,
    45, 47, 149n.12. *See also* "Coop"
De Crevecoeur, Margaret, 20
De Crevecoeur, Wal, 24, 27, 41
Deer Song, 94, 99
Desert, challenge of southwestern, 92–93
Dewey, John, 6
Dickson (coroner), 120
Dobie, J. Frank, 47
Dorris, Adam, 155n.13
Dorris, Michael, 79, 155n.13
Downhill Racer (film), 70
Drinnon, Richard, 3, 124

Edwards, E. I., 47, 114
Edwards, Harold L., 52
Egan, Ferol, 47
Environment, centrality to Indians of, 5
Ethnocentrism: Indian, 5; as prelude to hate, 125
Ethnography: Chemehuevi, 15–16; crisis in American, 15
Ethnohistory, 134

Fetal alcohol syndrome, 155n.13
Fiction: nature of historical, 132; Willie Boy in, 37 (*see*

173

also Lawton, Harry; Non-fiction, Willie Boy in; *Willie Boy: A Desert Manhunt*)

Film(s): books into, 55; Indians on, 55 (see also *Dances With Wolves*); truth and historical, 132; Willie Boy in, 3, 54–71 (see also *Tell Them Willie Boy Is Here*). *See also* Westerns (films)

Fisher, Adrian, 88, 96, 100–101, 105–107, 110, 127

Fisher, Edgar, 154n.1

Fish Vagina, 158n.24

Flores, Amelia, 96, 97

Fruit, of Banning area, 23

Ghost Dance, 15, 60, 97–101, 109, 111, 123, 134, 153n.8, 158nn.19, 24. *See also* Wovoka

Ghost shirt, 60, 61, 63, 71

Goulding, James, 73–74

Guerre, Martin, 14

Guthrie, James, 18

Hall, Harwood, 89

Harrington, Awonawilona, 90, 92, 95

Harrington, Carobeth. *See* Laird, Carobeth

Harrington, John Peabody, 89–90

Hertel, George, 52

Historians, dilemma of American, 4–7, 15, 145n.1

Hogan, William, 47

"Holden, Bill," 45, 77

Holt, Thomas, 18

Homosexuality, Indians and, 158n.24

"How Cottontail Rabbit Conquered the Sun" (folktale), 102

"How Wildcat Brothers Recovered Their Hunting Song" (folktale), 16

Hughes, Tom, 37, 38, 39, 91

Hyde, John, 24, 25, 27, 29, 33, 35, 41, 46, 118–20, 122, 149n.8

Indian Albert (Willie Boy ward), 101
Indian Bill (Willie Boy ward), 101
Indian-hating, 16, 35, 53, 85, 125, 126, 128–31, 134; in Banning, 74, 129; Christianity and, 13; Hollywood contribution to (see also *Tell Them Willie Boy Is Here*); by Indians, 12, 131, 154n.21; justification of, 36; Madison and, 91; metaphysics of, 3, 11–13, 50, 55, 80, 129–30, 134; in press, 19, 81, 84; as western U.S. myth element, 44. *See also* de Crevecoeur, Ben
Indians. *See* American Indians
Intellectualism, crisis in U.S., 145n.1
Irrigation, of Morongo Reservation, 23

James, Jesse, 154n.20
James, William, 6
Johnson, William E., 22
Jost, C. F., and family, 20, 21

Kael, Pauline, 69–70
Kennedy, John F., 69
Kennedy, Robert, 69
Kloppenberg, James T., 6–7
Knowlin, Joe, 27, 41, 121
Kroeber, Alfred, 90

Laird, Annie, 108
Laird, Carobeth, 89, 91, 94–96, 108, 112, 158n.24, 159n.34
Laird, George, 89, 91, 93–96, 99, 108, 157n.13
Landers, Calif., 14, 126. *See also* Willie Boy Days
Lansford, W. Douglas, 52

175

Lawton, Harry, 8–9, 10, 14, 34, 36, 37, 40, 42–53, 56, 60, 66, 70, 72, 84, 110, 111, 131, 132, 155n.11; on Ben de Crevecoeur, 39, 131; Madison influence on, 34, 44, 46–47, 84, 91, 131, 150n.23; and Malki Museum, 131; research of, 73, 77–79, 87–88, 91, 160n.15; and True Report, 154n.2. See also *Tell Them Willie Boy Is Here* (film); *Willie Boy: A Desert Manhunt*

Legacy of Conquest (Limerick), 85

Leupp, Francis, 22

Limerick, Patricia Nelson, 85, 128

Liquor. *See* Whiskey

Little Big Horn River, 83

"Liz," 57–59, 61–63, 65, 66, 68, 82

"Lola," 56–57, 60–63, 66, 68–71

Lolita (Nabokov), 44

Lolita (name), 57

Los Angeles Daily Times, 19

Los Angeles Express, 19

Los Angeles Herald, 18, 19, 34, 40, 147n.16

Los Angeles Record, 19, 31, 33. *See also* Madison, Randolph

Lyttle, Patrick, 96–97

McInnis, Jim, 73

McKinley, William, 69

Madison, James, 32

Madison, Randolph, 19, 24, 32–34, 44, 84–85, 126, 129, 150n.23; and Indian-hating, 91; as Lawton influence, 34, 44, 46–47, 84, 91, 131, 150n.23; lineage of, 32, 91; as posse member, 18, 31, 76, 126, 149n.8

Magazines, Willie Boy in U.S., 52

Malki Museum, 49, 131, 151n.47

Malki Reservation. *See* Morongo Reservation

Marriage, among Chemehuevi, 92, 93

176

Martin, Calvin, 5–6, 7, 11, 112
Media. *See* Film; Print; Television
Melville, Herman, 3, 11, 129, 130. *See also* Indian-hating, metaphysics of
Mike, Carlota, 23–25, 35, 82, 83, 106–11, 113, 115–23, 127, 134, 145n.6, 159n.31; abduction of, 8, 30, 35, 38–40, 45, 78, 110–11, 114, 130, 133 (*see also* Rapist, Willie Boy as); appearance of, 120; death of, 8, 25, 33, 38–41, 45–46, 48, 100, 113, 114, 120–23, 149nn.8,12, 151n.33, 160–61n.15; sand message of, 38–39, 119, 130, 131, 149n.8. *See also* "Lola"
Mike, Isoleta. *See* Mike, Carlota
Mike, Lolita. *See* Mike, Carlota
Mike, Mabel. *See* Mike, Carlota
Mike, Maria, 24, 75, 106, 116, 117–18
Mike, Neeta. *See* Mike, Carlota
Mike, William, 23–24, 88, 107–109, 111, 113, 116, 118, 145n.6; death of, 8, 24, 30, 35, 40, 43, 45, 78, 102, 107, 113, 114, 116–17, 119, 121–22, 129, 130, 151n.33. *See also* "Old Mike" (*Tell Them Willie Boy Is Here*)
Miller, Frank, 153n.12
Mission Inn, Riverside, 65, 153n.12
Mojave Indians, 93, 127; homosexuality among, 158n.24
Mooney, James, 103
Moore, Frank, 48
Morongo Reservation, 8, 20, 21–22, 35, 129, 147n.11; bit film parts for Indians of, 60; Lawton concern for, 49; on screen, 57. *See also* Cahuilla Indians; Malki Museum; True, Clara
Mountain sheep, 94
Murray, David, 15–16
Mythology, western U.S., 42, 44; Indian-hating as staple

177

of, 44, 134; Willie Boy role in, 9–10, 14, 32, 35, 36, 42–43, 85, 134 (*see also* Fiction, Willie Boy in)
Myths, Chemehuevi, 16, 102

Nabokov, Peter, 95
Nabokov, Vladimir, 44
"Newcombe, Clem," 45
Newspaper Enterprise Association, 33
Newspapers. *See* Press
New York Sun, 80, 81
New York Times, 85
New York World, 80, 81
Non-fiction, Willie Boy in, 37–53. *See also* Lawton, Harry
Novick, Peter, 4–5, 6

Old Mike. *See* Mike, William
"Old Mike" (*Tell Them Willie Boy Is Here*), 59, 63, 68, 71

Paganism, as Christian concept, 12
Paiute(s): Chemehuevi and, 90–91; "customs" of, 33–34, 63, 91, 130, 131; Northern (*see* Paviotso Indians); white fear of, 32, 84; Willie Boy miscalled, 24, 33, 34, 44, 49, 133
Paiute (term), 90, 91
Parker, Horace, 14, 44, 46–48, 160n.15
Paul, Nina Howard. *See* Shumway, Nina Paul
Paviotso Indians, 98
Pawnee, 55
Payne-Aldrich Act, 65
Pearce, Roy Harvey, 3, 13, 132
Penn, Jane, 49, 50, 131
Pine, Jim, 39, 108, 115
Plains Indians, 98. *See also* Sioux

Polonsky, Abraham Lincoln, 9, 56–58, 60–64, 66, 68, 69, 71, 82, 91, 131, 132, 153nn.8,13; benefactions of, 49; blacklisting of, 54; thrust of, 72. See also *Tell Them Willie Boy Is Here*

Posse, vs. Willie Boy, 7, 8, 24–28, 31–35, 38, 39, 41, 43, 46–48, 52, 76, 113, 118–25, 129–30, 132, 160n.15; ambush of, 27, 28, 41, 46, 75, 113, 114, 122–25; on film, 10; glorification of, 9 (see also *Willie Boy: A Desert Manhunt*). *See also* Chino, Segundo; de Crevecoeur, Ben; de Crevecoeur, Wal; Hyde, John; Knowlin, Joe; Madison, Randolph; Reche, Charlie; Toutain, Joe

Powell, Lawrence Clark, 47

Pragmatism, historical, 6–7

Press, Willie Boy in, 7, 13, 18–35, 52, 80–82, 118–19, 121, 123, 130, 132. See also *Los Angeles Herald*; *Los Angeles Record*; *San Bernardino Daily Sun*

Print, Willie Boy in, 11. *See also* Magazines, Willie Boy in U.S.; Press, Willie Boy in

"Purple Boundary, The" (Shumway), 37

Racism: in California, 19, 22; Indians and, 13 (*see also* Indian-hating)

Ralphs, John, 26, 41–42, 121

Randolph family (Va.), 32

Rape, white terror of Indian, 37

Rapist, Willie Boy as, 25, 33, 37–38, 40, 119

Rat Penis, 157n.13, 158n.24

"Ray," 57, 60, 62

Rebel without a Cause (film), 62

Reche, Charlie, 24, 25, 27–28, 32, 45, 74, 120, 149n.12; and Ben de Crevecoeur, 47, 76; wounding of, 27, 29, 40, 123; as writer source, 38, 39, 41, 46. *See also* "Coop"

Reconstructions, historical, 55, 56, 70–71. *See also*

Romances, historical
Redford, Robert, 3, 9, 10, 57, 70, 82. *See also* "Coop"
Redlands (Calif.) *Daily Facts*, 19, 33
Redlands (Calif.) *Daily Review*, 19
Relativism, historiographic, 5, 6
Riverside (Calif.) *Morning Mission*, 19, 80–81
"Robles," 77
Robles, Teofilo/Tefflie, 155n.11
Rogers, Dorothy, 87–88
Rogers, Sam, 73
Romances, historical, 55–56
Ross, Katherine, 9, 57, 70. *See also* "Lola"
Runners: Chemehuevi, 94–95, 98–100 (*see also* Rat Penis; Willie Boy, as runner); Indian, 95

Saint Louis Post Dispatch, 85
San Bernardino County (Calif.), prisoners of, 29–30
San Bernardino Daily Sun, 18, 19, 30, 33, 79
Saubel, Catherine, 110
Science, history as, 4–5
Shoshone Indians, 91
Shumway, Nina Paul, 37–38
Sioux, 55, 60, 98. *See also* Wounded Knee, massacre at
Skip (journalistic device), 28
Smiley, Albert K., 21
Smith, John, 99–100
Snyder, Mary, 106, 107, 121
Songs, of Chemehuevi, 93–94, 97, 99–100, 134. *See also* Ghost Dance
Southern Fox, 90
Southern Pacific Railroad, 20
Spirituality, American Indian, 10
Stevens, Bonita, 96, 97
Sullivan, Barry, 57

Sweeters, Clem A., 156n.14
Sweeters, Otto, 77–80, 131, 155–56n.14; father of, 156n.14

Taft, William H., 7, 29, 43, 60, 64–65, 69, 80–82, 133
Television, *Tell Them Willie Boy Is Here* on, 10, 70
Tell Them Willie Boy Is Here (film), 9–10, 14, 49, 54, 56–71, 85, 91, 110, 131; Cahuilla Indians in, 131; Chemehuevi "review" of, 110; factual weaknesses of, 65–66; Taft as "character" in, 82. *See also* Polonsky, Abraham Lincoln; Redford, Robert
Thief, Willie Boy as, 8
Time: anthropological vs. biological, 5, 11, 16, 112; Indian concept of, 5–6, 11
Toutain, Joe, 24, 41, 44, 47; on Willie Boy, 74, 130–31. *See also* "Coop"
Toutain, Lucy Ann, 21
Trackers, Indian, 7, 8, 24, 50, 118. *See also* Chino, Segundo; Hyde, John
True, Clara, 22, 28, 76, 83–84, 91, 108–109, 119, 121, 147n.11, 160n.11; agricultural accomplishments of, 23; vs. bootleggers, 22, 30–31, 66, 75, 153n.12; and Carlota Mike, 82–83; persona of, 22, 66; on Willie Boy, 73, 89. *See also* "Liz"
True Report, 154n.2
Tuska, Jon, 55–56, 62, 70, 132
Twentynine Palms, Calif., 23, 92; Willie Boy in, 26, 46, 102. *See also* Chemehuevis, of Twentynine Palms

Ute Indians, 91

Van Fleet, Alberta, 100–101, 105–106, 110
Villa, Pancho, 52

Waco, William, 107

Water, of Morongo Reservation, 23

Westerns (films), 55–56, 62, 63

Whiskey: Indians and, 36, 79, 98, 155n.13, 158n.19; on Morongo Reservation, 21, 30, 75 (*see also* True, Clara—vs. bootleggers); in Riverside County, 153n.12; Willie Boy and, 8, 30, 31, 35, 38, 40, 45, 57, 58, 74–75, 77–81, 102, 114–16, 126, 129–30, 133. *See also* Bootleggers

Wild One, The (film), 62

Williams, Walter L., 158n.24

Willie Boy, 7; appearance of, 103; background of, 88–89; Cahuilla cooptation of, 48–51; in Chemehuevi version of tragedy, 113; commercialization of (see *Tell Them Willie Boy Is Here*; *Willie Boy: A Desert Manhunt*; Willie Boy Days); as convict, 29, 66, 102; cremation of, 32, 33, 48–50, 114; death of, 8, 32, 34, 40, 46, 50, 100, 114, 123, 125; "escape" of, 100, 107, 113; mother of (*see* Snyder, Mary); as potential presidential assassin, 29; reputation of, 31, 37, 39, 72–74, 76–77, 80, 91, 115 (*see also* Whiskey, Willie Boy and); as runner, 95, 97, 101, 109, 111, 113, 119, 121, 127; wards of, 101; whites' memories of, 72–83, 88–89, 130–31; wife of, 107, 108. *See also* Blake, Robert

Willie Boy: A Desert Manhunt (Lawton), 8–9, 13–14, 42–51, 82, 85; kudos for, 47. *See also* Lawton, Frank

Willie Boy Days, 14, 52–53, 152n.54

Wilson, Frank, 42, 69

Wolf, Eric, 135

Women: Chemehuevi treatment of, 92; Indians and, 91; in Westerns, 62

Wood, Willard S., 38

Wounded Knee, massacre at, 60, 83, 98

Wovoka, 98, 100–103, 115, 127, 134, 158n.19